About Quicklook

OFTEN taken
cised, the "
great challenges and pressure to adapt to a
fast changing world. Society depends on the police to
protect people, property and our way of life.

This book covers all main aspects of police work.
We see how the police service developed, how political and social trends have influenced it and its relationships with the public. It is no longer realistic – if
it ever was – to think of "the public" as one group.

Quicklook
b o o k s

We examine the enormous range of tasks that the
police are asked to undertake, including crime prevention, detection and the prosecution process. There
is responsibility for the protection of individuals,
sometimes at vast events, or demonstrations – even
riots. Emergencies, such as natural disasters, require
police action. Apparently routine activities, such as
traffic policing, pose their own problems.

The different roles of uniformed and plain clothes
officers are explained and the relationship between
them is examined. There are many specialists in the
police. We find out what they do.

The police have for many years been early adopters
of technology. This continues to transform the way in
which policing operates – we find out how.

Police forces in the UK range from the huge
Metropolitan Police Service to much smaller county
forces. We see how they are structured, what the different ranks are and what officers at different levels
do. The recruitment, promotion and training proce-
dures are explained. There are many opportunities for
careers in the service – many of them for civilians.

We get inside the system and see how police stations function over a typical day.

Quicklook at

Police

Ian James

Published by Quicklook Books Limited

Weighbridge House, Grittleton SN14 6AP

First edition in e-book format 2011

This revised edition first published in hard copy 2012

Copyright Quicklook Books Limited (Company number 06641038) 2012

Cover photo from istockphoto.com. Photograph by George the Fourth

Books in the Quicklook series are available in hard copy and as e-books from www.quicklookbooks.com

Contact info@quicklookbooks.com

Printed and bound by CPI Group (UK) Ltd, Croydon, CR0 4YY

Quicklook is a registered European trade mark (number 008147258)

ISBN 978-1-908926-14-2

Contents

One   Why do we need the police?   7

Two   The development of the police   11

Three   Policing in a changing society   19

Four   The police and society   29

Five   Organisation of the police   35

Six   Uniformed police   41

Seven   The CID   47

Eight   Equipment and support services   55

Nine   The work of a police station   67

Ten   Recruitment, training and careers   73

Eleven   Major challenges   77

Twelve   Prosecuting offenders   85

Thirteen   The future   89

Where to find out more   92

About the author   93

More titles in the Quicklook series   94

Chapter One
Why do we need the police?

PEOPLE are not perfect. They have their own opinions, aspirations and qualities. They can be selfish, or worse. If they are grouped together in large populations, their conflicting wishes and actions can soon lead to friction, or conflict. Laws are needed to try to prevent this. All societies have them. They vary a great deal but have certain things in common. One of these is that, without a system of enforcement, laws are useless.

Certain types of conduct challenge the smooth operation of society so much that they are illegal everywhere. Murder, rape and other forms of unjustified assault come into this category. No society can in practice allow people to simply take whatever they want whenever they feel like it. As a result, theft is always a crime.

As the modern world has developed and populations have increased, more and more laws have been introduced to regulate what is regarded as unacceptable behaviour. These laws are useless if there is no way of finding out who has been breaking them and then dealing with them effectively.

Societies, including modern ones, are unattractive places when systems of law enforcement break down. The collapse of a government, as a result of invasion or revolution all too often leads to a period of looting and destruction. All of the things normally taken for granted, such as food, water and power supplies, can break down very quickly. Prompt and sometimes very brutal action is normally taken to restore order. In the meantime people take the law into their own hands – perhaps by forming vigilante groups in an effort to defend people, homes and property.

Life before the police

Laws, detection and punishment pre date the development of police. In the case of the UK, government and administration once depended on a hierarchy of powerful individuals. Starting with the monarch at the top, effective power was handed down to noblemen, who were normally major landowners with extensive powers of control over the people who lived in their areas. They, in turn, often relied on more junior, but still powerful, individuals to ensure that their interests were protected.

This feudal system combined supervision of local administration with the ability and obligation to raise troops in time of war or unrest. These were frequent occurrences and as a result the wishes of the local Lord or Duke could be enforced by armed soldiers and others, if required. There was certainly no power vacuum.

One of the more creditable aspects of the development of British society is that, for many hundreds of years, there has been a system of courts. These deal with issues of guilt or innocence as well as a wide range of "civil" disputes – which are cases which normally do not involve crimes at all. Many of the features of modern legal systems taken for granted today developed in England and Wales over hundreds of years. The system that emerged – the "Common Law", has stood the test of time and has been adopted by many countries around the world, such as the USA.

Features of the Common Law include independent judges, the presumption that the accused is innocent, until found guilty, legal representation for the accused and for serious offences, jury trials. A jury consists of a number of members of the general public. Their job is to decide whether the accused person is guilty or not. This is not done by the judge.

For centuries the Common Law operated in a rather rough and ready fashion. It was far from perfect – and is not perfect now. It did however achieve some very important things. Everyone, even the sovereign, was subject to the law. No one could do whatever they wanted. Certainly not the police, or the predecessors of the police.

Before the development of a professional police force, reliance was placed on private citizens, sometimes supervised by a local "Magistrate": an unpaid person with some judicial powers. Even today, private individuals have the power to arrest offenders. The elements of modern policing were in place. The police are drawn from the general population and have powers derived from those that everyone enjoys. These have, over time, been extended and almost all arrests are now done by the police, but the fact that they are "citizens in uniform" can still be important. They are certainly themselves very much subject to the law and their actions can be and regularly are challenged in the courts.

The legal safeguards that we take for granted do not exist everywhere. They are largely absent in a so – called "Police State", where police have few restrictions on what they do. In extreme examples of such societies, individuals can disappear in the middle of the night, never to be seen again. Dictatorships can use police to maintain a rule by fear and to remove people that they find inconvenient.

Policing, and the way in which it operates, has a huge influence on a society.

Chapter Two
The development of the police

Role of the police

THE task of the police is to enforce the law by taking steps to minimise crime and detect it and catch offenders when it occurs.

As society has developed, so has policing. This book concentrates on England and Wales, but many of the points which arise are of general application.

Sheriffs and Constables

Britain has for centuries been divided into administrative areas for local government purposes, called counties, or "shires". In Saxon times, over 1,000 years ago, the "Shire reeve" was an important local official, responsible for "keeping the peace", by a combination of acting as a Magistrate (in other words, a judge dealing with criminal cases) and supervising the arrest and processing of offenders. To this day Magistrates hold the title "Justice of the Peace".

Changes came about after the Norman Conquest but the names and roles of the "Shire reeve", or Sheriff, and Magistrates proved to be surprisingly enduring. Aspects of the old way of doing things persisted into the early 19th Century. Counties still have Sheriffs, but their roles are now largely ceremonial.

Sheriffs appointed one or sometimes more "constables". Their task was to arrest offenders for a wide range of offences, many related to poaching, theft, and robbery. These, usually unpaid, constables were drawn from their local communities.

The Industrial Revolution led to the rapid expansion of many towns and cities. The old way of policing, via unpaid part time constables, proved inadequate. Policing came increasingly under the control of police authorities run by the rapidly expanding local councils. As the 19th Century progressed, this led to the creation of a large number of local police forces. They were funded by both local and central government.

Robert Peel /Bow Street runners

The London Police Service was established in the 19th century primarily to counter the rise in crime after the Napoleonic wars. After the defeat of Napoleon at the battle of Waterloo in 1815 the army was reduced in size. Many soldiers returned home with little chance of employment. In addition many of those soldiers returned with injuries which made them unemployable. There were a lot of social problems, including plenty of crime.

Sir Robert Peel, who was Home Secretary in 1822, introduced the police constable to the streets of London in 1829. These officers were known as "Peelers" or "Bobbies" after their founder. They wore a long dark blue coat and a tall hat and this uniform made them stand out. The Metropolitan Police Act of 1829 set up the first organised police force for London, with 17 divisions, each with four inspectors and 144 constables. The force was controlled from Scotland Yard, and answerable to the Home Secretary.

In 1829 Sir Richard Mayne, the first Commissioner of the Metropolitan police, wrote:

"The primary object of an efficient police is the prevention of crime: the next that of detection and punishment of offenders if crime is committed. To these ends all the efforts of police must be directed. The protection of life and property, the preservation of public tranquillity, and the absence of crime, will alone prove whether those efforts have been successful and whether the objects for which the police have been appointed have been attained."

London was developing fast in the 19th Century and most of the population was living crammed into poor housing. This gave rise to all sorts of tensions and social problems. The newly emerging police forces certainly had plenty to do. Parliament lost no time in giving them powers to tackle crime. The view seems to have been that in those rough times, these needed to have wide scope.

Many of the laws introduced by Parliament in the 19th Century were still being enforced in the 1980's, especially in London. The Vagrancy Act of 1824 gave powers to constables to apprehend any person deemed to be a "rogue or vagabond" committing a wide range of offences that were obviously problems in their day. Many of the laws were enforced much more recently with reference to our modern way of life.

Common offences mentioned in the Act included *"persons pretending to tell fortunes, persons wandering abroad and lodging in any barn, or outhouse and not having any visible means of subsistence and not being able to give a good account of him or herself, exposing wounds or deformities to gather alms".* This law allowed police to arrest an offender who was known to police and was found out and about with intent to commit a serious offence. The law was so encompassing that any offender known to police could be arrested almost anywhere for being a suspected person. It became known as the "Sus" law. It was only repealed in 1981. It was widely regarded as creating a great deal of friction between the police and members of the public, particularly young (often black) men in urban areas, who regarded themselves as unfairly picked on or harassed.

Powers of arrest were soon increased further. Much emphasis was placed on the prevention and detection of theft. Then as now the law took a great deal of interest in protecting property rights.

From 1835 to 1856 two hundred and thirty nine police forces were established. There were borough council police forces, and county police forces.

Collecting Information: Criminal records

In 1871 the National Criminal Record Office (CRO) was set up, taking advantage of the new telegraph communications between forces. The system of recording criminal records remained unchanged for over 100 years. The guidance notes to police officers issued in 1965 reads: *"The Criminal Record Office at New Scotland Yard houses complete records of persons convicted of crime in the United Kingdom and can provide information about any of them to any police force requiring it, at short notice. It is a national registry of crimes, and a who's who of their perpetrators, a means of enabling new crimes to be traced to old criminals, and old criminals to be recognised with certainty when arrested. It is also the means of identifying a person by his 'trademark'."*

The booklet goes on to state that CRO must be treated as a BANK, which means simply that if you do not put anything in, you will not get anything out.

Creation of the CID

In 1877 the Metropolitan Police started the Criminal Investigation Department (CID), and by 1883 Special (Irish) Branch had been formed to counter the Irish National fighters known as Fenians.

Scotland

In Scotland the police service has been organised separately from those in England, Wales and Northern Ireland. The first known constables in Scotland date back to 1617. However the first burgh police forces were not established until the 19th century. An Act of 1833 enabled burghs to establish police forces. Counties gained the same powers in 1839.

There is a different criminal justice system in Scotland. In Scotland, the Procurator Fiscal decides on which cases the police should take to court. The courts are also different. This reflects the fact that Scottish law is much closer to European practice than the Common Law found in England and Wales. With separate laws, and a different criminal justice system, the Scottish police forces have their own training school, Criminal Record Office, and Police Authority.

Into the modern era

In 1964 the government decided to reduce the number of police forces in England, and Wales from 146 to 43. This was considered necessary to improve efficiency.

The Junior Home Office Minister (Lord Stonham) informed Parliament on 18 May 1966 that *"With the expert advice of HM Inspectors of Constabulary, I have carried out a review of police areas throughout the country. I have taken into full account of the recommendations made in 1962 by the Royal Commission on the Police; but I am satisfied that the continuing increase in crime and its changing pattern, as well as growing traffic problems, justify a more far-reaching reorganisation than was contemplated by the Commission. I have not thought it sensible to adopt any rigid formula for determining the right size of police forces, but I have examined each area and have sought to establish police forces of the size most likely to achieve full efficiency in the prevention and detection of crime and the control of traffic."*

Lord Stonham went on to explain *"These amalgamations would reduce the number of police forces in England and Wales from 146 to 43. I greatly hope that local authorities will recognise the need for these proposals and enter into voluntary schemes. But if they do not I must use my powers to promote compulsory amalgamations, for I am satisfied that these amalgamations are essential to a determined attack on crime."*

Needless to say the amalgamations went through. The new structure of the Police Service in England and Wales has stood the test of time. Of course the amalgamations met with some resistance to change and much complaint was made about the loss of identity arising form the creation of much larger police forces.

The Metropolitan Police ('MPS')

Of the 43 police forces in England & Wales, by far the largest is the Metropolitan Police (commonly referred to as "The Met" and more officially as the MPS). When I joined it in 1971 there were 21,000 police officers. Today the number is over 32,000, with about 15,000 support staff.

Some of the smaller county police forces such as Wiltshire and Northamptonshire have only 1,000 police officers. Although the policing objectives are very similar you cannot get away from the fact that the Metropolitan Police Service has greater responsibilities and resources, as the capital's police force. The scale and diversity of crimes committed in London makes it unique. They include complex white collar crimes. The special requirements of safeguarding the Royal Family, prominent politicians, diplomatic staff and other notables add to the demands. London is considered to be an especially attractive target for terrorists.

High fliers?: An Officer Class

In the 1930s Lord Trenchard, formerly an Air Marshall and by then Commissioner of the Metropolitan Police, introduced officer cadets. This was fiercely opposed by the Police Federation, which represents the interests and views of police officers. Specially selected officers, mostly from university, were trained at Hendon College and left with the rank of Inspector. The government of the day considered that an officer entry scheme was required for the police. Sir Robert Mark, (himself Commissioner from 1972-1977) stated *"The Hendon College, founded by Trenchard in the thirties, had produced some very good and some very bad policeman..... Hendon was established by Trenchard because, after taking up appointment as Commissioner he was appalled by what he found. His solution was to introduce into what had admittedly always been an artisan service, an officer class through a newly created college to be known as the Hendon Police College, which was intended to be rather like a police Sandhurst."*

The College was doomed, not because of an unreasonable hostility to an officer class but because as time went on it became apparent that it did not meet the requirements of police service. It is an occupation concerned with social issues. Experience in dealing with them at first hand as a constable is essential for the development of good, rounded, police officers. Classroom theory alone is not enough. In addition it was bitterly resented by the police service generally and by the Metropolitan Police in particular, because it limited the promotion prospects of those who were recruited in the ordinary way.

The police have always put much emphasis on experience, leadership and communication with people from all walks of life. Being street wise was something that could not be taught in the classroom. The formative years of walking the beat gave all officers the grounding for their future careers. However in the 1960's the police service introduced the "Special Course" for suitably qualified and recommended officers. This allowed for accelerated promotion to inspector. Those officers who had passed the sergeants exam and were recommended by their police force could attend a three day assessment at Bramshill Police Staff College in Hampshire. They were called, not without some envy, the "Bramshill Fliers".

The Special Course did produce some excellent senior officers who went on to lead police forces across the country. However there were many who found it difficult to live up to the expectations heaped upon them, and many never reached the rank of Chief Inspector. Much of the problem was ignorance within police forces on how to mentor and support officers with a great deal of talent. And of course there was still resistance from amongst rank and file to the idea of express promotion for these young stars.

Into the motorway age

It is interesting to note the importance placed on traffic policing in the 1964 Police amalgamations. The introduction of the M1 motorway brought problems for police forces situated along the route. The first part of the motorway went from London to Coventry via the M45, and this stretch of 100 miles was used by Jaguar to test the early E Types and the 3.4 and 3.8 Jaguar cars. It was reputed that the works cars could travel from Coventry to London in under an hour, with top speeds of over 120 mph. These cars were the favoured equipment of London criminals, who started using the M1 as a corridor of crime.

The Chief Constable of Northamptonshire Constabulary at that time was John Gott, a well known rally and racing driver. He was a works driver for the BMC team, driving Healey 3000s. He was well positioned to negotiate with Jaguar to provide his force with 3.4 Jaguar saloon police cars, modified to reach speeds of 130mph. Some of the excitement died down when the then (non driving) Minister of Transport, Barbara Castle, made the "experimental" 70 mph speed limit permanent in 1967. It has been in force since late 1965.

The motorway network also led to the formation of Regional Crime Squads to tackle "cross border" crime. In other words, crimes committed in one police area committed by those living in another. Teams of experienced detectives from county police forces were strategically placed to tackle organised crime, especially where firearms were used.

Chapter Three

Policing in a changing society

The 1970's

THE police service of England & Wales was moving from the Dixon of Dock Green image of the fifties through to the Sweeney era of the seventies. *The Sweeney* was a popular television series loosely modelled on the work of the famous London based "Flying Squad". (The name supposedly comes from cockney rhyming slang: Sweeney Todd – Flying Squad). Between the 1960's and the mid 1980's the Flying Squad acquired a formidable reputation as a specialist group of detective officers who combated serious and often organised (i.e. gangster based) crime in London. The contrast between their work and the perhaps overly soft and romanticised world of the friendly TV character George Dixon was stark.

Specialist teams were set up to deal with specific threats ranging from the Provisional IRA to organised crime. This stretched the underfunded and under resourced police. Police Constables in the early seventies were rather poorly paid. Many lived in section houses. These were effectively "barracks" for single male police officers. Married officers were provided with married quarters, but very few officers owned their own property.

The Thin Blue Line: shortage of officers

The Metropolitan Police in the 1960's and 1970's was undermanned. Despite having a theoretical establishment of 28,000 officers, the number employed was always well below this. It averaged about 21,000.

In order to cover their core duties, officers were required to work an additional three days a month. These were known as Additional Rest Days worked. On average, an additional 60,000 man days of work was provided each month. These resources allowed the service to work effectively against challenges like the Provisional IRA bombing campaign at that time. One notable success, among many which were less publicised, was the pursuit of an IRA team to Balcombe Street, where they went to ground in a flat and were later arrested.

Changes in working practices introduced as part of the Edmund Davis Report into policing in 1979 saw better working conditions for police officers and an increase in salary. When that occurred the Metropolitan police and other forces were able to recruit up to their respective establishments. However reductions in the time worked left them short of effective man days. Fewer officers were available for patrolling. The police embraced the use of vehicles to reach emergency calls within the agreed national target of 12 minutes.

Police officers no longer lived in section houses in central London, which often allowed them to walk to work. Those hostels often had 200 police officers living in single man quarters. There were three in central London. Police officers could not afford the property prices in London. There was a relaxation in the limits of where police officers could live. The old concentration of officers, able to assemble quickly in the event of an emergency, was heavily diluted. It can now take several hours to call officers in, as opposed to just minutes a few years ago.

The issue of manning levels is a problem that continues to this day. Consideration needs to be given to the question of what is the correct balance between police officers and civilian support staff. There are a lot of "sharp end" activities that can only be done by police officers.

'Bobbies on the beat'

At the start of the 1970's many police officers still started their shift in the time honoured manner. There was a "parade" before they went out on their patrol. This involved an inspection by the sergeant in charge to make sure that everyone was properly dressed and equipped, followed by a briefing as to the patrols to be done and any relevant information about what was going on and things to look out for.

This procedure, based on a significant amount of foot patrol policing, would have been recognisable by Sir Robert Peel. It is a policing method favoured by many today. There are regular calls for "more bobbies on the beat". A visible presence of uniformed officers can act as a deterrent to wrong doers. It can reassure the public. Because officers on foot are easy to talk to, they may gather useful information. They are well placed to get to know their local area, and the people in it, well.

Foot patrolling is still done but the early 70's marked the start of its decline, as resources were diverted elsewhere.

The police service throughout the seventies was severely tested by a changing society. Challenges were being made against "the establishment": in other words, the institutions of government and the old way of doing things. Trade unions were becoming very powerful. The country saw the "winter of discontent" in 1979, when there were a great many high visibility strikes affecting many services, including refuse collection. There was rising unemployment, which increased social tensions. The emergence of the Provisional IRA posed a serious threat to mainland Britain. Organised crime was on the up. The police were stretched to breaking point to cope with ever increasing demands.

What should the police service do to match their limited resources to the demand? The Panda car was introduced to speed up responses to incidents. Specialist teams were established to fight crime.

The Special Patrol Group

In London the Special Patrol Group ("SPG") was formed to spearhead the response to the IRA, organised crime, and serious public order problems. Four units of the SPG were formed – one for each Area of the force, commanded by a Chief Inspector. Each Area could muster 150 constables, and from the whole force 600 constables, many of whom were firearms trained, very fit, and experienced police officers.

It was an elite team of people who could have a positive effect on any police division. The reputation of the SPG was further enhanced when two patrolling constables in 1974 discovered a transit van parked outside New Scotland Yard packed with explosives. Had that vehicle exploded it may well have destroyed the communications centre for the force, and killed and maimed many hundreds of people in the Victoria Street location. It was their experience and diligence that saved the day.

The SPG had a high profile and its role in dealing with public order issues meant that this group of tough officers found themselves at the sharp end when often highly charged public demonstrations took place. The death of the demonstrator Blair Peach at one of these in 1979 led to much criticism and triggered enquiries which in due course led to the disbandment of the SPG.

IRA Terrorism

London and many of the cities in England and Wales became targets for the IRA. Police Constable Stephen Tibble was shot pursuing an IRA terrorist and others were severely injured. Bomb disposal expert Roger Goad lost his life defusing a bomb in Oxford Street. Improvised Explosive Devices (IEDs) were placed in public places to cause the maximum casualties, and incendiary devices were placed in major department stores. The IRA was at war with London.

Christmas in the seventies and early eighties was a busy time for policemen and women. Not only did crime go up as the criminal went out to get his or her presents by unlawful means, the IRA would carry out a bombing campaign to disrupt and frighten the public. Operation Santa was held annually to flood the West End of London with police to deter, and hopefully catch the terrorist delivering his bomb.

On 6th December 1975 four IRA terrorists fired automatic weapons into a restaurant in Mayfair, and decamped. The area was saturated with police and the pursuit led the four to Balcombe Street, where they went to ground in a flat occupied by two elderly residents. After a heavily publicised five day siege they surrendered.

The early days of advanced technology

Towards the end of the 1970's the police started to embrace technology. From then on, all patrolling police officers had radios. The traffic division in London swelled to 1,200 officers to free the flow of traffic and to tackle the increased theft of cars and the anti social behaviour shown by some drivers.

The Metropolitan Police had one of the first computerised command and control systems to manage the ever increasing number of 999 calls to New Scotland Yard. An airline ticketing software application was redesigned to record 999 calls and offer suitable units for deployment. Built by Unisys in 1977, it was eventually rolled out to all divisional control rooms by 1987.

This command and control system is still in service today in 2010, albeit much modified.

Industrial disputes

The changing role of the police service started to emerge in the 1970's. The use of the police force to keep open Grunwicks, a photographic development company in London, saw the Metropolitan Police pitched against pickets attempting to prevent non union workers going to work. Violent clashes occurred on the picket line outside the factory. Then in 1978 the Fire Brigade went on strike and the police service was called in to escort the Green Goddess fire engines (manned by the armed forces) to emergency calls.

The 1980's

The Miners' Strike

In 1984 the police were asked to help keep the coal mines open throughout the United Kingdom, as the National Union of Miners attempted to blockade mines and disrupt the transport of coal then so vital to the country's power industry. For the police service it was a grim time. Police officers who were part of the community were pitched against friends, in what was to become a political struggle between Arthur Scargill, leader of the NUM, and the Prime Minister, Margaret Thatcher. A national coordinating centre was set up, and police resources were bussed around the UK in military fashion.

Police officers would be away from their families for weeks, living in aircraft hangers, sleeping on camp beds and working 12 hour shifts. It was an operation that eventually broke the strike. It was from that point that the police service became regarded by many as a partisan instrument of the government. In many quarters that could not be forgiven.

The Brixton riots

The Brixton riots in London in 1981 were the worst riots of the 20th century. Robbery, burglary, and theft from cars were a major problem in the Borough of Lambeth in London. The police from Brixton conducted "Operation Swamp", which increased the numbers of officers on the streets of Lambeth in an attempt to counter the young criminals who were committing over 400 robberies a month. The money from the robberies was used to set up drug dealers, and so the cycle of violence and crime was perpetuated. Drug dealing on the streets of Brixton was open and blatant.

The method used to reduce this crime wave was an intensive stop and search operation, which inevitably antagonised the youth of Brixton. On 10th April 1981 officers were called to a robbery where a black youth had been stabbed. Believing he was about to be arrested, he broke away from the police who were attempting to administer first aid. The police restrained him and called an ambulance. His friends returned, attacked the police and took him to hospital by car.

Rumours spread that the police had inflicted the injuries, and the rest is history: 299 police injured, and at least 65 civilians. 61 private vehicles and 56 police vehicles were damaged or destroyed. 28 premises were burned, and another 117 damaged and looted. 82 arrests were made. Petrol bombs were thrown at police for the first time on mainland Britain and all that the police had to defend themselves were dustbin lids. The Special Patrol Group was re deployed and some 400 officers of the SPG, supported by local officers, restored order over a period of 48 hours.

The Brixton riots and the Broadwater Farm riot in north London, where PC Blakelock lost his life, gave rise to deep concerns about conditions in inner cities and the relationship between the people living there and the police. A detailed investigation by Lord Scarman, a very senior judge, produced a clear report of the course of events and triggered much thought about how such situations could be avoided in future. This may have had some success. There is still a great deal to worry about in deprived areas.

The riots and other tensions in what was a fast changing society led to a strategic re-think of the way in which policing should operate.

A new approach to policing

The 1980's brought a more liberal approach to policing. Questions were asked about how the police operated, and the media became more interested in operational effectiveness. The spotlight fell on how police managed public order events, investigated major crimes and the criminal justice system.

The 1980's was a time for change; it is probably the most important time for the police service during the 20th century. Police forces rebranded themselves as providing a "service" to the public; hence the Metropolitan Police Force became the Metropolitan Police Service. Management speak and reorganisation became the norm. In fact it was continuous change during that period.

"Performance indicators", budgeting, and "participative management" were just a few of the new management tools introduced to police forces. A more inclusive approach gave more junior officers a greater opportunity to make suggestions about their work, somewhat diluting the traditional "command and hierarchy" model. The late 1980's saw the police service undertake a review of managing all aspects of its work. The word "targets" appeared in management reports, and "staffing issues" became "human resources issues". The police service embraced modern management theories and looked to "rebrand" police forces. Many police cars changed colour from blue to white, and technology was put at the forefront of policing.

The Repeal of the 'Sus' Law

The calls for the repeal of laws that had seen the test of time, and had been instrumental in removing many offenders from the streets, were orchestrated by the many members of the local and national political parties. Ted Knight, leader of Lambeth Council, was outspoken in his opinion of police operations in Brixton, and was rarely supportive of them. Street crime was a major threat to public safety towards the end of the twentieth century. If there had been no repeal of the (admittedly controversial) "Sus law", then the police may well have had the powers needed to deal with many of the crimes committed today. Some argue that the scope and vagueness of the law and suspicions (justified or otherwise) as to how the police used it did more harm than good.

Modernisation

Out went the 1950's style switchboards with cables and bobbing eyes for extension numbers, and in came new style phones. Radios were becoming more reliable and every officer had one. Training was seen as key to improved performance. Computerised command and control systems were developed to manage the ever increasing number of emergency phone calls to the police, and computerised crime reporting systems started to evolve.

The 1990's

The 1990's saw a steady consolidation of the changes and technological improvements since the early 1970's. By the end of the decade there had been a transformation.

CCTV started to be introduced to the streets in a serious way and the use of computer based systems increased significantly. Prompted by the Home Office, efforts were made to standardise and harmonise practices and information systems across the 43 forces in England and Wales. These were not entirely successful and efforts continue.

The MacPherson Report

The high profile murder of the black youth Stephen Lawrence in London and criticisms of the effectiveness of the subsequent police investigations led to a wide ranging enquiry into them by Sir William MacPherson, a High Court judge. The findings that they were "marred by a combination of professional incompetence, institutional racism and a failure of leadership by senior police officers" made uncomfortable reading. 70 main recommendations were made and these have received much attention since.

No police officer wishes to see any offender go free after committing a murder. The unit dealing with this dreadful offence was already dealing with a number of murders. Its efforts failed to get a conviction at court. However many years later two of the suspects were convicted at a rare second trial, after DNA evidence provided a new impetus to the case.

There was much focus on the assertion that the police were "institutionally racist" – which was denied and strongly resented by many serving officers. It is certainly a bold and unpleasant claim to make against a service with many tens of thousands of individuals within it. Nonetheless enormous effort has been made to address the underlying issues. A House of Commons investigation, ten years after the original report, found considerable progress in many areas. Approximately 20%

of officers in the Met are now drawn from ethnic minorities. This represents a dramatic increase and, at least so far as London is concerned, certainly fulfils one of Macpherson's key recommendations.

The British tradition is that the police are "of the community which they serve". It is important that in an age where many "communities" are spoken of that police are drawn from them. If police are perceived as "outsiders", their work is very difficult.

Into the 21st century

Information technology was to lead to a faster delivery of service to the public, and the access to information from a number of sources. The old criminal record office at New Scotland Yard had been replaced by the Police National Computer in the 1970's. Over 20 years it was developed into a superfast database, holding millions of records on criminals, stolen property, plant, and motor vehicles. This was accessed over the radio through the police control room for many years.

Recent developments have seen this information now accessed through mobile technology in cars, and hand held devices. The rapid development of these, such as the Mobile Data Terminals in cars and iPads, offers exciting prospects to the police. They will increasingly have formidable computing power at their disposal while on the move. This may offer solutions to long outstanding problems, such as the rapid transfer of information between police forces.

Many activities undertaken by police forces have now been outsourced to private companies to remove the financial risk and cost from the individual police force. Vehicle maintenance, management of information technology and radio systems are just a few of the functions now managed by organisations not normally associated with the police service.

As the police service moves into the 21st century it has become more accountable. It is dealing with work which is so diverse it bears little relationship to the work completed by Sir Robert Peel's "bobbies". The core business of answering 999 calls and deploying a resource (not necessarily a police officer) is still very much the same, but those employed in specialist departments now outnumber officers delivering the core police service.

Chapter Four
The police and society

THE success of the police service in the UK relies heavily on the support given by the public. The majority of police forces in the world are based on the military. Their rank structure reflects that and police are armed as a matter of routine. In mainland UK (but sadly, not in Northern Ireland) the normal practice is for police officers to be "unarmed", which really means "without a gun".

Some say that these approaches reflect varying philosophies in relation to policing, or at least a different emphasis. The "military" approach leans towards the role of the police as an organ of the state, "defending" it against "attack" by the public, or at least its less cooperative members. The British approach can be described as one of "citizen police" based in the community, who help society in general as a "service". Whether there is a real difference is a matter for debate. What is much clearer is that the police can do their work most effectively when the public trust them and are happy to help.

Relations between the police and public

The police service polices the people by consent, and this has been the long standing philosophy of British policing. We have a police service that reflects the society of the day.

What is 'the public'?

It might once have been sensible to consider the position of the police with reference to "the public", but it would be inappropriate to do so now. These days there is much talk of "communities". Society is divided into very diverse groups, identified by ethnic origin, nationality, age, sex, religion, political views and other factors. There can of course be combinations of these.

Second generation "immigrants" can have a very different view of life from their parents. For one thing they are not immigrants. They are often exposed to very differing influences as traditional conservatism, associated with general behaviour and personal relationships, comes up against what can seem to be the breathtakingly liberal, or immoral, British way of doing things.

At the time of the 2005 London bombings the then mayor of London, Ken Livingstone, pointed out that London is home to more than 160 nationalities, speaking about 200 different languages. It is hardly surprising that there is no standard view of the police. Those who have come to the UK from elsewhere may have a very unfavourable instinctive view of how policing works.

Causes of tension

Many issues can cause people to think of their relationship with the police in terms of "us and them", rather than "we".

Laws

One of the things that the police have to do is enforce the law, whatever it is at the time. There are more and more laws to deal with. Some of them create friction, or worse, with people who might be generally very law abiding. Most people accept the need for motoring speed limits but many are less than keen if these are robotically enforced via speed cameras regardless of circumstances. Controversial fox hunting laws seem to some to be tailor made by town dwellers to criminalise people who live in the country. Even laws banning the use of cannabis are offensive to those who claim that it is not really different from the readily available (drug) alcohol.

It is not clear that law makers give much consideration to the effect that law has on relationships with the police. If these are damaged, police work becomes more difficult.

Media

The media concentrate on what is newsworthy. A quiet day in a pleasant town is not. A rowdy demonstration, riot or police misbehaviour is. So is an unsolved murder. Even if unintentionally, a bad impression of police behaviour and competence can be created, simply by reporting news.

Other agencies are at work in society which target the police much more directly. Those who want to achieve dramatic change often see the police as the embodiment of the system that they want to attack. In the internet age it is easy to spread anti police views, or invented rumours, which can exert considerable influence and are very hard to counter. This is not at all new. Back in the 1960's the emerging "counter culture" produced numerous "underground" publications which routinely portrayed the police as the enemies of society.

Culture

Language, religion and culture can create huge barriers. Loyalties to a "community" or group may be much more powerful than the impulse to assist the police, even when the group itself disapproves of the crime being investigated.

In the case of Irish, or Islamic, terrorism there may be sufficient sympathy with the aims, if not the actions, of the guilty parties to enable them to shelter within a community, protected by a wall of silence. This can, of course, sometimes be strongly reinforced by fear of the terrorists.

Sometimes people want to take matters into their own hands instead of dealing with the police. Some follow a code or value system separate from and sometimes in conflict with the law of the land. (The treatment of women is one area where this occurs.) Huge resentment can be created if, despite the obstacles, the police seek to enforce the law in such circumstances.

People matter

The old fashioned model of policing relied upon a visible presence of uniformed police on the streets. In addition to the deterrent effect of this it provided regular opportunities for the personal contact with the public so vital to effective police work. Views of "the police" can change dramatically when they have a human face. Personal contact can be an excellent way of gathering information, including background intelligence which can trigger useful enquiries. Individual officers can acquire a detailed and thus important knowledge of their area and the people within it.

New methods which reduce this mean that the police service is losing the ability to communicate with the public. Recently there has been an emphasis on the introduction of community policing teams. There is a strong view that these will need to return to the original policing ethics of preventing crime, and the preservation of law and order. This is the core business requirement of the police service, and the use of technology and "process" must be secondary. It is policemen and women who will win the battle against crime, not computers and paperwork. However cutbacks in police numbers may see this form of policing shrink, with more emphasis on the reactive role of the police officer.

Politics and the Police

For many years the police service was left to undertake the primary objectives of the police: the protection of life and property.

There are areas where threats from within are perceived as more damaging to the country. Both World Wars focussed people's fears on agents spying for Germany. Internment was a method of restricting the movement of people perceived to be a threat to the nation. The police were used to detain and transfer "enemy aliens", as they were then known. Even as recently as the 1970's aliens registration forms were completed by those nationals whose movements needed to be kept in check. Part of the associated conditions was a requirement to sign on at police stations daily.

Strikes

The rise of trade union activism in the 1960's and the associated fear of communist influence brought successive governments into conflict with the trade unions. A three day working week, brought about by a miners' strike, was implemented in 1974, followed by an election which resulted in a change of government.

The Fire Brigade strike in the late 1970's was particularly notable because it involved one of the emergency services. Such was the determination of the then Labour government to break it that the army was engaged, with old "Green Goddess" fire engines. Care is taken to avoid confrontations between the army and the public and these were given police escorts. The strike was discontinued. This was the start of using the police in the political arena, and in the following years the police would be used by Government at times of severe industrial unrest.

The Grunwick film processing plant in London dismissed a large number of union members of staff who had been on strike. The company then employed non union staff to fill those jobs. The trade unions drew heavily on their resources, and picketed the works, attempting to close the factory. Police were engaged daily to keep the gates open to allow the staff to attend their place of work. The situation was often ugly and violent. This factory was picketed by union members from elsewhere, a practice which became known as secondary picketing. This was eventually out-lawed, but only after serious public disorder at many places of work.

The Miners' Strike of 1983-84 brought miners' leader Arthur Scargill in direct conflict with Prime Minister Margaret Thatcher. Some viewed the struggle as a question of "Who runs Britain?" in view of the fact that a miners' strike had led to the fall of the government ten years earlier. It was certainly widely felt that the strike had a strong political dimension to it. Police officers from across the UK were mobilised. Many saw this as a political move designed to break the strike.

A national coordination centre was established in London to manage the thousands of police officers engaged at coal mines across the country. Police officers stayed away from home for up to four weeks at a time. Violent scenes were seen on television screens as pickets attempted to prevent miners attending their place of work. After a bitter struggle the strike effectively collapsed. This was the last time that the police were used in such large numbers in connection with a strike.

The damage to police and public relations in the pit villages and towns was huge and bitterness still extends today through generations. The impartiality of the police is paramount to policing and the lesson learnt from this strike is that the police should only be used in political disputes only as a last resort.

One thing that the police and the armed forces have in common is that they are not allowed to take legal strike action. It has never been attempted. It is the police, not the army, who have to cope with difficult, even extreme, confrontations on the streets, whether because of industrial action or, more commonly now, political demonstrations.

Improving Relationships

Considerable emphasis is now placed on actively trying to improve relations between the police and the public. Visits to schools enable officers to contact the young. Community police officers regularly write advice and information columns in local publications and liaise with neighbourhood watch teams, where these exist. (These provide a structured way of communicating with those who live in an area.) Sometimes attempts are made to hold "surgeries" at which local people can speak to an officer. They are not always well attended.

Some police forces have very active (and expensive) in house civilian Public Relations experts. The aim is to secure awareness of what the police do and to effectively present the police perspective on newsworthy events. In the case of sensitive enquiries and prominent investigations this can be a very important and skilled exercise. The help of the public can be asked for and is often invaluable. The popular "Crimewatch" TV programme is a prime example.

Chapter Five

Organisation of the police

Political control of the police service

THE Home Office has responsibility for the police service and it works closely with the Police Authorities for each force. In most of the country each force comes under its own Police Authority, whose membership is made up of local councillors and a few other individuals. The Metropolitan Police Commissioner (who has Britain's top police job) reports to the Metropolitan Police Authority (MPA). This body is made up of a mixture of elected members of the London Assembly and other appointed individuals. The elected Mayor of London has responsibility for the authority and considerable influence over it. The last two Commissioners (Sir Ian Blair and Sir Paul Stephenson) left their jobs earlier than expected. Between them they served for about three years. London has now had four Commissioners within a four year period, following the appointment of Sir Bernard Hogan-Howe in July 2011. It seems clear that one of the many things that holders of this very important post must have is the continuing confidence and support of the elected Mayor.

There are suggestions that other police authorities could in future be headed by locally elected individuals, as happens in parts of the USA. The idea is that this would connect the community more closely with the police. It is debateable whether the British system, with its large police districts and lack of any tradition of political campaigning for such posts, would comfortably accommodate it. There might be considerable variations between different police services in their allocation of priorities and resources, making cooperation and rationalisation harder to achieve.

It will be important for the Police Service to remain politically independent. Senior police officers must be allowed to carry out operational decisions without political interference. The introduction of regional police commissioners may bring this about, and such a proposal needs careful evaluation.

At present, although each Police Authority has overall responsibility for each police force, the chief officer has full operational command and makes all decisions on operational policing.

Ranks and command structures

Of 43 police forces in England and Wales 42 have a similar rank structure. The remaining one, the Metropolitan Police Service, has a rank structure which is unique.

The Metropolitan Police Service ('MPS')

The Metropolitan Police Service is the largest police force with over 32,000 police officers, 15,000 civil staff, plus Police Community Support Officers and Special Constables who provide additional support.

The Commissioner of the MPS has a deputy, and four Assistant Commissioners. There are then a number of Deputy Assistant Commissioners responsible for operational areas and departments. Their deputies for this organisational structure are Commanders. All of these ranks are unique to the MPS.

A Borough Command Unit (BCU) is an area aligned to a London Borough, to allow for easy contact with the local community and its leaders.

A Superintendent or Chief Superintendant leads a team of usually two or three Chief Inspectors, who have operational responsibility for key areas within the BCU. The management roles will include head of the Criminal Investigation Department (CID), head of uniform police operations, and head of Human Resources, although in some areas this is undertaken by a civilian member of staff, as employment law has become so complex.

Inspectors are the front line leaders, managing the day to day deployment, supervision, and operations on the BCU over a 24 hour period. Although the Inspector oversees the daily running of his team, the Sergeant on the team is the key to the success or failure of any policing initiative. This is because the roles of everyone above this level have a strong emphasis on management and administration, particularly in the uniform branch. There will be normally three to four Sergeants per shift to motivate, and direct Constables and Police Community Support Officers (PCSOs). At the larger BCUs each Sergeant could have a dozen officers under his command.

PCSO's

(Police Community Support Officers) are not police officers and do not have their powers of arrest. Introduced in 2002, their role is to assist the police and provide a supplementary presence of (cheaper) uniformed personnel. It is hoped that this reduces anti social behaviour and generally helps to provide contact with the public, which has been reduced as police officers undertake fewer foot patrols. Although this represents something of a return to the idea of "citizens in uniform" being involved in law enforcement, there is controversy about their effectiveness. Some argue that the money would be better spent on the recruitment of more police officers.

Special Constables

These officers have a much longer history than PCSO's. They are unpaid volunteers, who work part time and have the same powers as regular police officers. In September 2010 there were nearly 17,000 "Specials" across the UK – slightly more than the total number of PCSO's.

Other police forces

The 42 Police Constabularies have exactly the same command structure up to the rank of Chief Superintendent. Above that rank there will be three or four Assistant Chief Constables, and in some larger forces a director of finance, human resources, and communications. The Chief Constable heads up the Constabulary with a Deputy. These senior managers are known as ACPO officers, which means that they are members of the Association of Chief Police Officers. In addition to their day job they will normally have a national role to undertake. Examples are the national strategy on domestic violence, traffic enforcement, terrorism, and police information technology.

The size of police forces varies across the country, with the big city forces such as the Greater Manchester Police having several thousand police officers, and the smaller county police forces such as Wiltshire and Northamptonshire having about one thousand officers.

Organisation and administration

Each police force has a team of people to support its operations. They are all sizeable, complex organisations with large, if stretched, budgets. The following departments are required to enable a police force to run effectively. All of them will have staff who are not police officers:

● A Human Resources Directorate

● Strategy and Improvement

● Finance

● Procurement Services

● Property Services

● Business Systems and Integration

● Training

● Forensic

● Legal Services

● Directorate of Public Affairs and Communications

● Technology

● Transport

There are increasing pressures to reduce the 43 police forces to a smaller, perhaps more manageable, number. This has been strongly resisted by Chief Officers, citing local accountability, and a loss of identity. Recent moves to bring about local amalgamations have been side stepped. However chief officers are conscious of the advantages of economies of scale, and the joint purchasing of vehicles, helicopters, uniforms and fuel are new initiatives being undertaken.

National Police Bodies

SOCA

A number of national organisations counter serious crime. Some years ago there were Regional Crime Squads, which comprised teams of officers from several forces. They were set up to deal with "cross border" crime, i.e. investigations which covered several police areas. Now the UK police service has the Serious Organised Crime Agency ("SOCA"). This group works closely with all police forces, and is resourced with experienced officers. The teams work closely with Customs and Excise and drug operations are one of the main activities of the Agency. The large returns on investment from the sale of drugs in the UK have provided top criminals with large profits. SOCA can operate anywhere in the country. Its role is in some ways comparable with the Federal Bureau of investigation ("FBI") in the USA.

The Independent Police Complaints Commission

This took over the functions of the earlier Police Complaints Authority in 2004. It is responsible for investigating complaints against the police and makes enquiries into such things as the use of firearms by the police. Although it has its own staff, the investigations are normally conducted by local police forces working under its supervision.

The task of investigating other police officers is a difficult one, even when it is dealt with by members of a force from elsewhere, which is the norm in all sensitive cases.

Chapter Six

Uniformed police

Uniforms

THE 70% or so of police officers who belong to the uniformed branches carry on the tradition of wearing distinctive dress which started with Sir Robert Peel's constables in the early 1800's. Traditional and now somewhat old fashioned helmets are instantly recognisable and rather iconic. They identify the police in much the same way as wigs identify barristers or white coats identify hospital doctors. Not all forces still use helmets. Peaked caps are the norm in some areas, notably Scotland and for some specialists. Traffic police wear flat caps with white tops.

Basic police uniforms are a very dark blue colour (also strongly identified with the police). This is often now combined with bright "High Visibility" clothing when appropriate. Constables and Sergeants, but not more senior ranks, display a number on their shoulders which is unique to them in their force (or Division, in the case of the Met). All uniformed officers in the Metropolitan Police now wear name badges. Some other forces (such as Greater Manchester) have also adopted this approach.

Uniforms can confer authority on the person wearing them and the presence of someone clearly identifiable as a police officer can have a deterrent effect. People are unlikely to commit offences straight in front of someone who might obviously arrest them as a result. Uniforms can also fulfil much the same function as football kit, by making it clear which individuals are police officers in crowds or even riots.

The distinctive appearance of the police is regarded as important. It is an offence to impersonate a police officer, e.g. by wearing similar clothing with the intention to mislead.

As with any organisation there are many specialists. The police service in the last forty years has spawned many different departments, many in response to a particular threat or crime that has to have the appropriate police response.

Beat officers

Officers who conduct foot patrols ("beat officers") operate as the backbone of policing. Their numbers have declined considerably over the years. Once regularly seen, especially in town centres, they are now almost a rarity in many places and virtually never seen in country areas.

One of the biggest problems facing the police with respect to specialist departments is that the bobby on the beat is not considered "special". He or she works shift work, often with only one weekend off a month, and they are the front line police officers taking all the abuse and violence. Efforts have been made over the years to give the career constable the support and a career structure that has been needed, but sadly little has been achieved. "The Bobby" is the first point of contact with the public, and provides the core response to 999 calls. It is an important and demanding job requiring a good knowledge of the law and the ability to communicate. As such it is very rewarding work, but often underrated by many senior police managers.

Traffic police

With increased traffic on the roads, and the construction of the motorways in the 1960's, police forces introduced Traffic Divisions to enforce the Highway Code and traffic regulations. Traffic police are often first at the scene of accidents involving injuries or even death. More recently the Highways Agency is normally first to the scene of a motorway accident, as the police have reduced their presence on motorways. In addition to making sure that other emergency services respond appropriately, prompt action on the scene can be needed to make the road safe and to preserve and gather evidence of how the incident occurred. Criminals regularly use vehicles and another key role is to stop and search vehicles suspected to have been involved in crime.

From the early days, traffic officers were readily identified by the white tops to their caps: the first evidence of Health and Safety in the police service. Distinctive uniform also served as a reminder to the motorist that he had been stopped by a professional who knew his traffic law, and therefore should be treated with the greatest of respect. In the days when cars were not as mechanically well constructed as they are today a traffic patrol officer could always find a fault with a motor vehicle or motorcycle, whether it be defective steering or a badly worn tyre. It was therefore unwise to be impolite to a traffic officer, as you could find your car with a PG 9 notice, which meant it was too dangerous to drive, and the poor driver and his passengers left to walk or get a taxi home.

Traffic Patrol sergeants were even more powerful within the police force, having the power to relieve police drivers from driving duties at the scene of an accident. All accidents involving police drivers in a police vehicle were reported and investigated by Traffic Patrol sergeants. Where there was evidence that the police driver was at fault, the sergeant could relieve him from driving duties forthwith. Traffic Divisions across the country grew, with police officers being trained to the highest standards of driving, and motorcycling. The highest standard is "advanced car driver", or motorcyclist. Most of the bread and butter work of traffic patrols was done by motorcycle. A key priority in the 1960s and 1970s was to keep the highways free flowing. Often traffic junctions would have to be policed in the morning and evening rush hour. At times this involved directing the traffic by standing in the road and giving signals to drivers: something that has become rare. As computerised traffic signals evolved those fixed traffic points disappeared.

Traffic police are experienced police officers before they are accepted into the Traffic Department. The motor vehicle is still the favourite mode of transport for criminals. An experienced officer can assess the occupant(s) of a vehicle, the type of vehicle, and now check it against numerous databases before deciding whether to stop it. Any vehicle can be checked for compliance with what are now very complex laws governing their condition. Drivers and vehicle licences, plus insurance can be checked. While this is being done an officer has a good opportunity to size up the situation generally. If his hunch is correct he will find a host of other offences connected to the people in the car. The stopping and searching of vehicles is still bread and butter policing for Traffic Patrols for detecting breaches of Road Traffic Regulations, and the possession of stolen goods, drugs or offensive weapons.

Improvements in the design and reliability of motor vehicles, coupled with the rigorous MOT testing system, have reduced concerns about the road worthiness of cars. Speed and other traffic cameras have been introduced, thereby automating some aspects of enforcement. In recent years the number of traffic officers has reduced. On motorways, members of the Highways Agency (who are not police officers) now perform some of the functions done by the police, including the management of traffic following an accident.

The British Transport Police

This specialist force has a long history – dating back to 1826, in other words, at the start of policing in its present form. It operates throughout the UK. It has about 3,000 officers and 1,500 support staff, with a London based HQ and stations throughout the UK. It has a wide range of capabilities including a (plain clothes) CID department.

The role of the transport police is to police and protect the railway system, including the underground. The force has been at the forefront of the development of CCTV, now widely used on railway stations and also on trains. It can investigate serious crimes and was heavily involved in coordinating the response to the terrorist bombings in London on 7/7/05.

Other special departments

Marine Policing

In the Metropolitan Police, the Thames Division was one of the earlier departments formed to counter the thefts from barges on the Thames. Of course they had the unenviable task of fishing dead bodies from the river. Sadly over the years there have been many of these. The river Thames is a fast, navigable, highway. Long used to convey goods and people, it required policing both to maintain safety on the river and also to deter criminals from robbing ships, barges and other craft. Today the marine police in all police forces have the responsibility for preserving life, and the prevention of theft on the waterways.

Mounted police

As large, powerful animals, horses are of value in helping to control crowds at football matches and demonstrations. A specialist team of officers is trained in this role. However they are of course police officers and can and do conduct patrols on horseback and respond to emergency calls.

Police dogs

Dogs are rarely deployed on crowd control duties, although when present in the background they can have a deterrent effect. It is the animal's acute sense of smell and the fact that dogs can easily be trained that is of most value. Dogs are regularly used to sniff out the presence of drugs or explosives.

Dogs are especially useful in searching for people. They can be deployed in searches for missing persons, sniff out people who may be hiding, perhaps in a concealed space, and pursue suspects. At night their sense of smell enables them to stay on the trail of someone trying to run away.

It is difficult, if not impossible, to outrun a police dog. They are able to tackle armed individuals – thereby reducing the risks faced by their human handlers.

Chapter Seven

The CID

The Development of the Criminal Investigation Department ('CID')

THE Special (Irish) Branch, known today as just Special Branch, was set up to counter the threat from Irish Nationalists in 1833. This was the earliest dedicated team of officers set up to collect intelligence and respond to threat to the mainland from Ireland. These officers infiltrated the Irish community and for many years attended meetings reporting back to Scotland Yard on their activities.

It became clear that there was considerable advantage in having a number of officers working in plain clothes. It is not always a good idea to advertise the fact that enquiries are being made. Even such activities as following a suspect become much more difficult in uniform. Covert investigations are almost impossible to do in uniform.

It was recognised that police forces needed officers to undertake major investigations such as murders, robbery and extortion and that plain clothes officers should undertake these roles. The Criminal Investigation Department ("CID") was set up to investigate such serious crimes. These officers learnt a great deal on the job. Training was not something that police forces emphasised in the 19th century. A tradition grew up of knowhow being passed down within the department. Knowledge was power, and the CID developed a culture of keeping things within the one department, which in turn led to it having a very elitist mindset. There was little movement back to duty in uniform. Once an officer had been accepted into the CID it became his family and it was a very tight knit association.

The role of the CID

The CID has responsibility for investigating all major crime. In London, each Borough Command Unit (BCU) has a team to investigate local crime. Officers in the CID normally undertake enquiries discreetly and also undertake surveillance operations. Crimes not investigated by the CID are passed to uniform officers working their beats. Crimes investigated by BCUs range from motor vehicle crime, the theft of and theft from motor vehicles, theft, burglary, and local drug offences. The more serious offences, such as murders and rapes, are investigated by specialist teams.

Locally the CID undertakes the investigation of crime. Working in plain clothes, the team has the opportunity to target local criminals and cultivate informants to obtain information. Where support is required to counter a rise in a particular crime the BCU can call upon other resources to support this initiative. In the Metropolitan Police the Territorial Support Group provides experienced officers to flood an area to detect and arrest offenders. Each TSG team consists of an inspector, four sergeants and 30 constables, normally split into three teams. These officers are trained in surveillance, public order duties, and searching techniques. The TSG team will normally support a BCU for a month to six weeks. All police forces run similar units to provide a mobile support function to BCUs and to respond to major incidents.

Outside London different forces offer mutual support to each other as required to deal with a major or unusual investigation. The riots in London in 2011 saw this mutual aid called upon to deal with over 20 spontaneous riots across the capital.

The tradition of exclusivity remains. CID work is regarded as specialised and movement between the CID and uniform branches, while far from unheard of, is rare. All police officers start in uniform and selection to the CID can come after three or four years of uniform duty. The CID in some respects still sees itself as an elite group. Some move from uniform to the CID at the rank of Inspector. After undergoing training in CID work they then spend a few years in the CID in order to get a complete grounding in all aspects of police work. This is a favoured path for those expected to attain high rank later in their careers.

Working patterns for CID officers are different from their uniformed colleagues. It can involve early and late shifts quite often, which is attractive to some. Night working and unsocial hours are less onerous than for those in uniform. With more weekends off, working conditions are more favourable than their uniform colleagues normally experience.

Specialist departments

Specialist departments provide much needed expertise. However over the years some become dependent on just a few officers, and an air of elitism occurs. Rotation of staff through departments is both healthy for the force and helps career development. A balance has to be struck. The merits of accumulating expertise by keeping people in the same roles have to be weighed against the dangers of corruption if there is never any movement. Things can get "too cosy" as relationships build. This is an ever present cause for concern in the police, whose work, inevitably, involves a considerable degree of contact with criminals.

Across police forces there are numerous specialist departments to deal with problems that have developed over the years. The difficulty that the police face is the ever increasing sophistication of criminal activity. To respond to this they police have to find the expertise and resources to tackle it and cope with an ever increasing work load. As a result, front line response policing has been steadily reduced to provide resources to counter the threat from terrorism, drugs, robberies, public order events, firearms offences, murder, domestic violence, serious sexual assaults and vice.

The diversity of the police service means that it offers a wide range of attractive career options. However this has eroded the thin blue line. The continuing development of specialist departments has robbed front line policing of many experienced officers. A radical rethink may be required on how police resources are deployed to achieve greater efficiency. Smaller police forces are now combining specialist departments across regions to make better use of their staff. Such initiatives include joint Special Branch units, drugs units, and others. Specialist departments are essential. The police need to keep one step ahead of the criminal., Proactive and often covert policing, using a wide range of technology, is having significant success against serious crime.

Gathering evidence

Much police work, especially for the CID, involves the assembly of evidence. It can take many forms. Gathering it has to be dealt with very carefully. Criminal courts operate to a demanding standard of proof, well beyond the "balance of probabilities" test applied in non criminal cases. The police have to find, record and preserve high quality evidence.

Where necessary they can be empowered to enter premises and seize articles which might prove to be evidence. This is normally done by the issue of a search warrant by a magistrate. Grounds for the associated invasion of privacy have to be given, but is rare for police requests for such warrants to be refused. An arrested person may have his/her premises searched under S18 of the Police and Criminal Evidence Act.

Witnesses

First hand witness accounts from reliable people can be of great value. Tracking down those able to provide such evidence is not always easy. Conducting interviews to find out what they know is a skilled task. It may be necessary to reassure them about the process before they feel able to talk freely. In difficult cases steps may be needed to protect witnesses. Repeat interviews may be needed as an investigation develops.

The sooner evidence from a witness can be recorded, the better. Memories of events can fade or become confused remarkably quickly. Because of this it has long been the practice for police officers, who are often themselves witnesses, to carry a notebook. Something written down in that within an hour or two can count as very convincing evidence of an incident. In the modern electronic age old fashioned written reports still have considerable value. There are problems with electronic notes, partly because electronic material is so easy to alter.

One important area is identification evidence. At one time "identification parades" were quite common. The suspect lined up with a number of members of the public. If one, or, ideally more, witnesses picked him out this was convincing, if not necessarily conclusive, identification evidence. There were considerable problems in organising such "parades". Suitable and willing members of the public could be hard to find, particularly if the suspect was of unusual appearance or ethnic origin. The integrity of the process required a line of people of roughly similar age and appearance. Quite often volunteers for identification parades were almost impossible to find.

Other approaches are now commonly used. In London, escalators in tube stations can be useful. The suspect travels up the escalator with other members of the public. If a witness picks him out of the crowd, this is persuasive evidence.

Personal searches

Those who are arrested and taken to a police station are routinely searched. Their belongings are taken from them, recorded and placed in bags. Their home may also be searched. Great care is taken to eliminate opportunities to hide or dispose of incriminating material, such as stolen goods, drugs or a weapon.

Crime scenes

Physical evidence can be very important and this can include the scene of the crime itself. This may show damage, signs of a struggle, motor vehicle skid marks or tyre tracks, foot prints and additional evidence at the scene itself. This may disappear (e.g. if it rains or if a road is reopened). Prompt investigation can be needed to record the scene. Sometimes this results in considerable inconvenience to the public, such as closed roads or motorways.

Vital objects and other forms of evidence, such as blood and DNA, can be found at a crime scene, and elsewhere.

Special "scene of the crime" officers, who are civilians, carry out investigations and try to find vital clues. The site is secured and made the subject of careful steps to avoid contamination. It may be necessary to collect evidence, such as fingerprints, of the normal occupants of a property in order to eliminate these and identify those left by an intruder.

Speed is often vital. The first hour at the scene of a crime is regarded as "the golden hour".

Objects

A blood spattered hammer may be an important piece of evidence. If so, it will undergo a carefully controlled journey from the place where it was found to the court room. Every detail will be recorded, starting with where and when it was found, who found it, what happened to it at every stage thereafter, what tests were made and what was discovered as a result.

The "chain of custody" evidence is crucial. If it does not hang together, the object may not be admitted as evidence at all. The officer finding the article will exhibit it and be responsible for producing it at court.

Documents

Crime can take a great many forms. Evidence of it can be found in all sorts of documents, especially in cases of business related crime; often called "white collar" crime. Bank statements and other records may contain vital information.

Computer and electronic evidence

"Documents" are often to be found on computers. Once something has been generated electronically it is very difficult indeed to completely erase it. Simply pressing a "delete" button is unlikely to achieve this. It is often possible to retrieve material from a hard drive even after quite vigorous attempts have been made to over-write it. Even physically damaged discs can still reveal their secrets. As documents move around within an office or over the internet, multiple copies can be created. Internet Service Providers can provide all sorts of information about who has sent what and when.

The ever increasing importance of the internet and digital material provides opportunities for gathering evidence secretly. This is the digital equivalent of phone tapping, which is another productive source of information. There are numerous concerns about the invasion of privacy involved. However these techniques can be invaluable in detecting and in some cases preventing serious crimes, such as terrorist bombings.

Advanced techniques need to be used with care. Revealing their details can be counter productive to other operations. Where other evidence is available the prosecution may not rely on evidence collected by them.

CCTV

Closed Circuit television ("CCTV") cameras are now to be found in almost all of Britain's town centres and anywhere else where many people gather or there is a strong risk of crime (such as some housing estates). They are to be found on private land and in many shops. They monitor traffic on motorways and other major roads and are widespread on the rest of the transport system. Britain may be more "observed" than any other country as a result.

Not everyone is happy with CCTV. It is, however, a very rich source of information and can provide evidence of people's movements and much else. Premier League footballers rarely commit fouls that are not spotted by a TV camera. The presence of CCTV cameras on our streets does not achieve the same in relation to crime, but it is perhaps getting a bit closer to this as the system of CCTV cameras develops.

The approach of the police when faced with widespread rioting in the 2011 riots in London was influenced by this. The MPS was certainly taken by surprise at the scale and widespread nature of the disturbances, which were encouraged and to some extent arranged via the mobile phone network. An overly forceful reaction might have worsened an already bad situation. The police know that there is such a wealth of CCTV, media, and phone images that the vast number of people involved in such situations will be photographed in the act of committing a crime, and can be arrested at a later date, usually with the proceeds of crime at home. There were substantially more arrests for offences in 2011 than there were in 1981 at the Brixton riots, and far fewer police officers, or members of the public, were injured.

Expert evidence

Prosecutions can depend on the evidence of an expert. Experts are allowed to give "opinion" based evidence. Almost any subject can be covered. In criminal cases DNA, finger print, medical and handwriting evidence is often given by experts. Prosecution lawyers can sometimes be involved in helping the police to gather some forms of expert evidence. Defence lawyers sometimes call expert evidence, leaving the court with the difficult task of deciding which of two rival expert opinions is the correct one.

Chapter Eight

Equipment and support services

THE high standard of proof needed to secure a conviction has been a very long standing feature of British justice. Partly as a result, the police have often been early adopters of any technology, or piece of equipment, which can help to secure useable evidence. The gathering and analysis of fingerprint evidence, which can be vital in associating an accused person with a crime, is an early example. It remains very important and effective today.

Information systems

Interoperability is the key to successful policing, and clear communication between departments and between police forces. The police service of England & Wales has been struggling to achieve this. In the last 40 years, the police service has embraced technology to such an extent that the UK leads the world in the development of IT systems for fighting crime. Although many police forces have looked to the USA for the lead, systems developed in the UK have generally been preferred. The key reason is that the British policing model is different. In America there are thousands of police forces, many of them small Sheriffs' offices with just a handful of police officers and police vehicles. Locally elected police chiefs can come and go at the whim of the public. Only the major cities show any similarity of approach to our metropolitan police areas.

Many positions formerly covered by police officers are now dealt with by civilians in an effort to save money and/or bring in new types of expertise. The aim is to allow officers to concentrate on the work that only they can do. For example, the majority of call handling staff in emergency control rooms are civilians. The number of police officers engaged on administrative duties has been reduced and retired police officers are being encouraged to stay on help the administrative burden of investigating minor crimes.

In England & Wales police forces are now considering outsourcing complex systems to organisations that specialise in information technology. Companies providing this service can achieve efficiency savings, by developing regional models which can be used by several forces.

National system?

In 1994 the Police Information Technology Office attempted to bring about a national programme for police information systems. Four key IT systems were identified which could become national systems for the police forces of England & Wales: Command & Control, which manages the 999 call handling and deployment of police resources, Case and Custody, Crime Reporting, and Human Resources. This process was called the National Strategy for Police Information Systems. All the systems were supposed to confirm to a common data model to allow for the exchange of information between systems and forces.

Contracts were negotiated for three of the systems, but they failed to achieve the transfer of data to a common data format. An opportunity for interoperability between police forces was lost, as chief officers, fearful of amalgamations by the back door, resisted change. The Home Office has always faced the difficulty of having 43 powerful leaders, and trying to bring them to agree on a national strategy for police information systems in 1994 was ambitious. In addition to the 43 chiefs there are 43 directors of IT. Any national system threatens their decision making power as to which IT systems to purchase for their own force.

There are changes on the way. The National Police Improvement Agency (NPIA) is insisting on more open systems to encourage more efficiency and a more economic process in purchasing IT systems.

Scottish police forces have embraced a national strategy for information systems through its own organisation (Scottish Police Information Systems). Scotland has moved to a national command and control system which will enable operational interoperability between police forces. Sadly this operational benefit will be missed by police forces in England and Wales.

Police forces are now seeking to outsource some of the above activities, to improve efficiency and to take advantage of leading edge technology. Information Technology and radio services are two of the key areas. They can be shared by different police forces.

Airwave

"Airwave" is the emergency service national radio infrastructure. Developed for the police service in the late 1990's, it is now the national radio system for the Police, Fire Brigade, Ambulance services and Coastguard. The difficulties encountered at 9/11 in America accelerated its introduction across the United Kingdom. It means that the emergency services can talk to each other at a major incident. The remaining gap in the operational capability for the police service is that there is no national command & control system, which means that data cannot be passed between police forces in emergencies.

The adoption of the Airwave system has been a successful implementation of IT, which has improved communication and officer safety and delivered good results. It now covers the London Underground system, which has improved the safety of the network and makes it easier for the British Transport Police to undertake operations.

The Airwave managed service offers police forces an opportunity to share technology with other police forces, because it is a national application. Economies of scale can provide big savings.

No national Command and Control system

One of the least successful IT implementations was the ambitious plan to introduce a national command & control system for the police service. In 1997 the Police Information Technology Office signed a contract to build it. This should have delivered a standard model for managing 999 calls and despatching resources. This is core police business. Implimentation of the system would have brought significant improvements to management of police resources, detecting cross border crime, and supporting the front line police officer.

The contract was with Securicor Information Systems and the system was built to manage 20,000 incidents an hour, and to have a sub second response to functional requests. The contract however was only for seven years, and police forces were not obliged to join in. In addition there was no financial support from central government to implement it. Chief Constables, suspicious of central control and given no financial support, failed to support this initiative. As a result, the police service in England now has several different systems, rather than a national one capable of operating seamlessly. This contrasts with the position in Scotland, which has a single integrated system.

'HOLMES'

One success is the "HOLMES" system (Home Office Large Major Enquiry System). This was delivered after the difficult "Yorkshire Ripper" investigation in the 1970s, which again highlighted the different methods of communication and investigation techniques used by different forces. This made investigation of "cross border" crimes (i.e. covering more than one police area) more difficult.

In a big investigation, the huge amount of data collected needs to be put into a major data base to allow for efficient searching. HOLMES has developed over the years and has been responsible for solving many major crimes. It is the detective's key tool for investigations which stretch across police forces and involve large numbers of witness statements and coordinated action by detectives.

The Police National Computer

In recent years the police service has been building intelligence databases. Some of these stores of information have not been able to communicate with each other. Specialist departments have been collecting intelligence and not sharing the information. Key improvements have been made which improve networks, connect information and allow police officers access to it through one source.

The Police National Computer (PNC) holds information on wanted persons, stolen vehicles and vehicle records. These include an insurance and MOT data base. It is the oldest national system that the police service operates. This information is now available to patrolling officers via mobile data terminals, and more recently hand held "Personal Digital Assistants" (PDAs). On the ground, police officers now have more technology available to them than ever. Radio technology was first introduced into the police service in the sixties. This succeeded Morse code, which was used after the Second World War in police vehicles. Mobile data is now provided to vehicles, which allows access to the Police National Computer (PNC) and to systems in police stations.

Information on the move: Mobile computing

Police vehicles are now designed as mobile offices, enabling officers to remain on patrol rather than return to the police station to complete reports or make enquiries.

The Greater Manchester Police has developed a vehicle with access to the force command and control system and intelligence databases which can access photographs of suspects. It has digital cameras at the front and rear of the car connected to the Automatic Vehicle Number Plate Recognition (AVNPR) system. This flags up stolen vehicles, or those which have no insurance or MOT. In board video cameras enhance officers' safety and record the actions of a prisoner in the rear of the vehicle. Many prisoners will attempt to conceal drugs and offensive weapons in the back of the car whilst being transported to the police station or whilst being questioned in the car.

The Wiltshire police service has also gone down the road of mobile computing, equipping vehicles with mobile data terminals to allow officers to access crime reports, command and control and intelligence data bases.

One of the major developments of Airwave radio has been the provision of a Global Positioning System. Control rooms can now track police officers on foot patrol and in vehicles. This provides control room operators with real time information on the position of all police units. This means that the most appropriately equipped vehicle can be deployed to attend the scene of an incident. It improves response times and officer safety. One of the key selling benefits to police officers is the emergency response button on the radio. If pushed, it sends an urgent signal to the control room, indicating that the officer requires urgent assistance and it will pin point his location through the GPS system.

Control rooms

A typical police force handles 3,000-4,000 "999" calls each day. In the case of the MPS the figure is about 15,000. At the time of the riots in 2011 the MPS received a record 20,000 calls in a few hours. The 999 number is intended to be used for emergencies. In the case of the police this includes threats to life, crimes in progress, cases where a member of the public is pursuing or confronted by a criminal and cases where the criminal is still near a scene and might be caught.

Now that most people carry a mobile phone, the volume of 999 calls has greatly increased. At least 70% of them are non urgent.

It is the task of the control room to react to 999 calls, prioritise them and manage the response.

In an effort to reduce the burden, a new number – 101 – is being introduced for non-urgent calls to the police.

Other technology

CCTV

CCTV has been expanded throughout the United Kingdom. Love or hate it the network of cameras does provide valuable evidence in the event of a crime. Many police forces are now connected to local authority CCTV systems, allowing remote operators a series of views of many town centres. The quality of pictures has now improved, which has allowed CCTV images to be used in evidence. There are national guidelines covering the implementation and the use of CCTV.

Although there are some people who object to the implementation of CCTV, there are many others who can see the advantages of the systems to make our towns and cities more secure. As with any advance in technology it is important to make sure that they are maintained and operational 24x7, and that those working in control rooms are properly trained.

Cameras are a visible deterrent. They often prevent crime, where they have been used identify criminals acting suspiciously at the scene of a planned crime, enabling police to intervene. In this way the "eyes" of the police have become much more efficient. For example, trouble brewing in a town centre late at night can be picked up and nipped in the bud before anyone gets hurt.

The British Transport Police is one of the leaders in the use of CCTV to search for the suspects of crime on the rail network. The majority of trains and stations are now covered by CCTV. Any crimes committed can be reviewed, and images published to identify the culprits. Typical crimes on the rail network include assaults and robberies. CCTV has been a great success in helping to identify and convict offenders.

Strathclyde Police, the largest police force in Scotland, has integrated 3,000 local authority cameras into their control rooms. This is helping to reduce anti social behaviour in Glasgow and the system has also proved invaluable in solving and preventing the commission of major crimes.

Speed Cameras

The Speed camera is probably the most unpopular system introduced into the UK. The redeployment of traffic officers to other duties has left the enforcement of speed limits to machines. Suspicions over the extent to which they are there for road safety rather than revenue collection have raged since their introduction. Cameras located at dangerous junctions, and at accident blackspots, have a legitimate purpose but the apparently indiscriminate placing of speed cameras caused significant damage to police-public relations. The police service relies heavily on information from the public to solve crime. Speed cameras have driven a wedge between the normally law abiding citizen and the police service. The recent decision to remove many static cameras, and reduce the number of mobile camera units, will be welcomed by many. Only time will tell if the speed camera was an effective deterrent to speeding, a cash cow for the government, or a bit of both.

Computerised mapping

Computerised mapping is now used to plan the use of police resources and to analyse crime trends with reference to areas. The improvements in this type of technology have allowed police forces to plan operations and brief officers in far greater detail. Crime area maps show where each crime is committed. This helps to identify trends and hot spots – resources can then be allocated accordingly. These maps are now being made available for public inspection. It remains to be seen what the effects of this will be.

The implications of the new technologies

Technology is now driving much of police business. There is a fear that police officers are becoming too reliant on information stored within systems, and not using their experience gained working in close contact with criminals and society in general.

Consider an example of relying too much on technology, rather than the officer's experience. A police patrol car is waiting in a service station car park when an armoured cash collection vehicle arrives on the forecourt to make a collection. A vehicle containing four men arrives, and their behaviour leads the officers to believe that a robbery is about to take place. The suspects see the police vehicle and leave the service station. Before moving off to challenge them the officers carry out a registration number check on the vehicle. After a short time the response comes back that the vehicle is on false number plates. With the vehicle gone, the officers have prevented a robbery but lost four major criminals who were about to commit it.

Technology should support police and not be used as a decision making tool. Too much reliance on technology will remove the discretion that police officers have to carry out their duties. The fear is that police will retreat to their highly equipped vehicle-offices and not get out and communicate with the public.

Police forces are now looking to keep police officers on the beat by issuing them with PDAs. These hand held computers allow access to the force command & control system, and various police data bases which will allow the officer to record crimes, and search the Police National Computer. The key driver for this technology is to reduce the paperwork police officers have to complete, and to keep them out of the police station. This initiative will help community policing teams to remain on patrol for longer and gather important intelligence for those officers in specialist departments to take proactive action against drug dealers, robbers and car thieves.

Firearms

The British police have a long tradition of not carrying firearms. This is one significant way in which the concept of them being "citizens in uniform" has a practical effect. Most other countries base their police forces on the military model. Firearms are carried as a matter of course, even by those who undertake generally safe tasks, such as checking passports.

The fact that most officers are unarmed makes British police more approachable. Guns are, obviously, intimidating. It is widely thought that criminals are much less likely to carry guns themselves. Carrying a gun does not always make the officer safe. Police who routinely carry them (e.g. in the USA) sometimes suffer as their weapon is taken from them in a fight and used against them. There is much to be said for restricting the issue of firearms to specialist officers who are highly trained in their use.

There is a great reluctance to involve the armed forces in any confrontation with the public. If there is an operational need for firearms, the police service has a number of specially trained officers to call on. One important trigger for the development of police firearms was the "Siege of Sidney Street" in 1911. This highly publicised incident involved police attempts to arrest a gang who had already killed police officers in their efforts to evade capture. A prolonged gun battle in Sidney Street in London only ended after the then Home Secretary, Winston Churchill, authorised assistance by armed soldiers. The incident led to consideration of how the police themselves could deal with such incidents in the future.

Criminals cannot be relied upon to obligingly go without guns all the time. This particularly applies to terrorists. To counter them there have for many years been specialist, highly trained, firearms officers. They undertake patrols and are in a high state of readiness. Their units represent an expensive resource. Specially adapted cars with gun safes patrol our streets, and where authority is given the officers can arm to deploy to an incident. There are strict rules of engagement.

Occasionally a member of the public runs amok, shooting people indiscriminately, or selectively, based on past relationships. This has happened in Hungerford, Cumbria and at a school in Dunblane, in Scotland. The difficulties involved in dealing with such incidents without injuring innocent bystanders are considerable. Split second, life or death, decisions may be required.

Sadly, the need for firearms is on the increase. They can be seen very visibly from time to time at places like airports, where it is necessary to deter and, if it comes to it, deal with, a terrorist attack.

Other weapons and equipment

Firearms officers may carry tasers, which administer a sharp electric charge which is disabling, but not fatal and can be used at short range. Beat officers have the Asp, which is the modern equivalent of the old wooden truncheon and also pepper sprays. They normally wear stab proof vests and carry handcuffs to restrain someone who is being violent.

The use of modern equipment and recent improvements in communication, which have made it easier to make an appropriate response to an incident (e.g. by directing the most appropriate unit) has reduced, but not eliminated, the old requirement that police officers must be physically formidable individuals. The old minimum height regulations have been abolished, to be replaced by a more general requirement that police must be fit and robust. Female officers, who make up about 20% of the police service, are deployed on general patrols and other duties which may involve violent confrontations.

Forensic services

"Forensic" means "concerned with legal matters". Forensic investigations to assist the police have been of vital importance for many years, particularly in relation to serious and/or hard to solve crimes.

Scenes of Crime Officers ('SOCOs') have been the backbone of crime scene investigation for over 50 years. In the 1950's and 1960's fingerprint evidence was the core evidence that they were able to deliver. All burglaries where marks were discovered were visited by a SOCO. In more complex cases pathologists and forensic science officers examine samples collected by the SOCOs. Carefully produced photographic evidence is often used.

The work of these, nearly always civilian, officers has considerably expanded over the years. They are trained to seal and preserve a crime scene and gather and preserve the evidence available at it. This is often of critical importance in securing a conviction at trial. The officers are regularly required to appear in court for this purpose. Their findings are provided to defence lawyers in advance. They may decide to challenge them with rival evidence or perhaps advise the defendant to plead guilty.

Material found at a crime scene, especially early on in the "golden hour", can be of huge importance in helping subsequent investigations, sometimes before the trail goes cold.

The National DNA Database has been a major tool in solving major crime. DNA is found in every cell of the body and is unique to each individual, just like fingerprints. It is difficult for someone, even a careful, experienced criminal, to spend time at a location without leaving behind tell tale DNA evidence. In cases involving violence and associated sudden activity the DNA of the aggressor may be retrievable – perhaps from the victim.

Since 1998, more than 300,000 crimes have been detected with the aid of the Database. Its use means that offenders are more likely to be brought to justice. Governance and oversight of the National DNA Database is provided by the National DNA Database Strategy Board.

A number of people want the DNA database restricted. At present it contains the DNA of over 10% of the population. Controversially, this includes not just the DNA of current suspects, or those convicted of an offence, but also those acquitted or not even charged at all. The case for retaining it in its present form, or something like it, is based on its great effectiveness in solving crime. There are many offenders being brought to justice after many years of avoiding detection. Often this is for the most serious offences.

Examples can be seen on the DNA Database web site. For more information click this link: www.npia.police.uk/en/8934.htm In 2010 Terence McVicar was sentenced to 20 years imprisonment for sexually abusing a four year old girl in 1990. The case was reviewed by the West Yorkshire Police's Operation Recall. A cold case review found a preserved hair on the victim which was found to belong to McVicar. Faced with this evidence, he pleaded guilty.

Another example of how powerful this database is to the police in solving crime is the case of Gavin Gordon, who was jailed indefinitely in May 2010 after being convicted of unlawful imprisonment, robbery, actual bodily harm, and theft. He was part of a gang that targeted a 26 year old woman and her partner in their Clapham home. Gordon was caught after his DNA was found on a drinks carton at the scene of the crime.

Pathology

This is a specialist branch of medicine. It covers the study of the human body and its tissues and organs. As we all know from suitably grisly TV dramas, it includes the examination of dead people for the purpose of deciding the cause and often the timing of their death. Much of the work of pathologists is connected with Coroners enquiries. The police assist Coroners, whose special Courts investigate all suspicious deaths.

Police doctors

Doctors are often required in connection with police work. They can be asked to ensure that those arrested are fit to be questioned and if necessary treat anyone who has suffered an injury, whether he be a suspect, his victim or a police officer. They are often known as Divisional or Borough Surgeons. In addition to the above duties they attend sudden deaths and suspicious deaths.

Doctors who undertake police work can expect to have to give evidence in court, e.g. as to the injuries suffered by an assault victim.

The position becomes most sensitive in cases of rape and other types of sexual assault. The examination of the often traumatised victim is essential if vital evidence, including DNA evidence, is to be obtained. Considerable efforts have been made to improve the treatment of sexual crime victims in police stations. The harsh fact remains that being the victim of a serious crime is very unpleasant. If justice is to be done then evidence must be collected. The establishment of serious sexual assault examination centres has greatly improved the treatment of those victims.

Other expert services

The police can and do use outside experts on a case by case basis, as do lawyers representing defendants. The range of possible subjects covered is almost endless.

Chapter Nine
The work of a police station

P OLICE stations are as old as the service itself, starting with the base for the famous Bow Street force. They are the centre of policing for a local area and something of a landmark – "the local nick". Like other workers, police need a base from which to operate and usually a desk, or access to one. Their base police station provides this and is therefore, among other things, their office. It is the office for quite a lot of civilian staff as well.

In the interests of efficiency, many smaller stations have been closed in recent years. Those that remain are of very varying shapes and sizes, ranging from the modern and functional to rather splendid, if sometimes outdated, Victorian structures. All of them announce their presence via the blue sign outside. Blue is very much a colour associated with the police.

All large stations operate for 24 hours a day, Bank Holidays included. In addition to office facilities, including the all important computers and telephones, they will often have a canteen. This serves those detained, in or visiting, the station as well as police and other staff. Police stations are an important contact point with the public, who may come in for all sorts of reasons, including reports of crime, real or imagined complaints about anti social behaviour, or to comply with bail reporting conditions or a request to produce evidence of motor insurance. The police also operate a "lost and found" service for mislaid property. Some honest people hand in wallets stuffed with cash, or other valuables. Reception facilities and the good humour of the station staff are required to deal with all comers.

Detention of suspects and gathering evidence

Not everyone entering a police station does so voluntarily. Arrested people, normally brought in by the back door, rather than the main entrance used by the public, first enter the charge room. A duty sergeant is responsible for the admission procedure. The identity of the individual is recorded on a computerised database. He is then searched and all possessions taken away. These are recorded as well. The records created by the process are now linked to the Crime Support Unit (which collates information and prepares the case papers) and the Crown Prosecution Service ("CPS"). The idea is that information now only needs to be entered once.

It is normal for arrested people to be questioned shortly after their arrival. They have an opportunity to make a phone call. As a result of this they may be accompanied by a solicitor, or some other person, in any interview.

Interviews are now recorded, sometimes via video as well as voice. They can provide evidence to be used in a subsequent court case.

The decision to charge a suspect

Criminal cases are based on one or more "charges". These are written down and briefly identify the law that is alleged to be broken and the conduct that amounted to the offence. In the past the decision as to what charge to bring was taken by the police, especially in more minor cases. All such decisions are now taken by the CPS.

Bail

It may take a considerable time before enough investigations have taken place to decide whether to bring a charge and what it should be. The law does not allow arrested people to be detained for more than 24 hours without an application being made to a magistrate. A magistrate may allow a further period of detention. Unless the police want more time for questioning, the police may be happy for a Court to grant bail. This is almost always subject to some conditions. The prisoner himself, and often another individual, faces a financial penalty if he fails to reappear when required. The process is called "granting bail". Generally speaking, Courts are reluctant to have people kept in custody. They are of course innocent until proved guilty. Once they have been charged most people are granted bail. Sometimes the conditions can be quite strict. They can include sizeable sums as security, regular reporting to a police station and the surrender of any passport.

The working day

Work patterns

Police officers and civilian staff work from the station, with police officers and police community support officers working shifts. In recent years there has been a move away from the traditional three-shift pattern of eight hour tours of duty to a more flexible 10 or 12 hour tour of duty. Officers now work four days on and four days off, quite often two day shifts followed by two night shifts. The advantage of this system is that physically the body does not get into the routine of either night duty or day duty. In the past officers worked three weeks of continuous nights with days off in those three weeks, and later went on to a seven night shift pattern of eight hours. Support staff and officers attached to the CID often work a day duty based regime. However, there are late shifts and night duty to be covered by the CID.

Setting off on patrol

A typical shift will start at 7am, with officers parading for a general intelligence briefing and posting to patrols. Traditionally officers presented their "appointments", to show the sergeant taking the parade that each officer had his notebooks, truncheon and whistle. Today the amount of equipment an officer carries makes this impractical. A foot patrol officer will typically carry a range of equipment including a steel extendable Asp, which has replaced the old wooden truncheon (which was a kind of club). There will be pepper spray, a PDA, note books, stab proof vest, and Airwave radio. Officers in the metropolitan areas may make foot patrols, but in rural areas they patrol in cars. Officers will book on to the force command and control system through the radio. This shows their availability for deployment.

Mornings

In the first few hours of duty in the morning officers will pick up calls from the control room for burglar alarm activations, as businesses open and accidently set off the alarm. Nearly all soundings of alarms are false alarms. Road traffic accidents during the rush hour are bread and butter, and are normally of a minor nature.

Most criminals are nocturnal animals, waking at midday and carrying out their activities during the afternoon and evening.

Afternoons

Burglaries on dwelling houses tend to be in the afternoon, when mothers are on the school run, or in the evening under the cover of darkness, when it is apparent if no one is at home because all the lights are out. Home owners are encouraged to have lights on a time clock if away from home.

The value of cars makes the theft of vehicles attractive to the professional criminal, who has moved away from armed robberies. A typical high value car can be worth £40,000 and sitting outside in the driveway. The criminal will look for an easy way to obtain the car keys, either by putting a metal rod through the letter box and hooking the keys, or by physically breaking in and taking them. Car keys should be kept out of view and reach of any door or window. A stolen car can be easily disposed of in Europe, Africa or the Middle East. They are often used as currency for drugs, which are then sold in the UK for a massive profit, and so the cycle of crime continues.

Such is the workload of police officers that unless the suspect is nearby an officer responding to a crime will attend only as soon as is generally practicable. This can often be by appointment, some days after the event, if there is no likelihood of any marks being found. The introduction of mobile computing for police officers will help to speed up the reporting of crimes. Members of the public are now encouraged to report crimes over the internet.

In metropolitan areas, organised shoplifters will work the shops, often stealing to order, drug dealers will emerge into the daylight and ply their trade from local locations, often stashing their goods in nearby walls, doorways, and gardens so that when stopped and searched they will have no drugs in their possession. If they are unlucky enough to be caught before the music stops they will normally only have enough for "personal use". If so they may just get a caution. In order to arrest these offenders a surveillance operation will normally have to be undertaken, to get sufficient evidence for a conviction for supplying drugs.

There has been an increase in growing cannabis in factories and even houses. This is where good community policing can pay dividends. In addition to information from the public the police have other tools to detect these drug manufacturing centres.

Theft from vehicles is still a major problem. Satellite navigation systems, laptop computers, iPods and mobile phones are easy targets for the criminal. The police continue to emphasise the importance of removing these high value items from cars or at least locking them in the boot. Many of these crimes are committed by an opportunist criminal walking the streets looking for such an opportunity. These stolen goods are often sold for drugs. This is a vicious circle as young people become dependent on drugs, and then they need an income to support that habit.

With fewer officers patrolling the streets, the opportunity to stop and search such offenders has diminished. Despite the repeal of the "Sus" law, stop and search remains a useful tool in the fight against crime. Police officers must now have reasonable suspicion that an offence is being committed or is about to occur. This gives considerable scope – possession of drugs, or a weapon, is an offence. Nowadays a record of all such searches has to be made.

The emphasis on collecting intelligence, targeting and surveillance has meant that specialist units have been established to respond to certain crimes. This is not a new initiative: police forces have had robbery squads, burglary squads, and drugs squads for many years. All of these units compete for intelligence and often work in isolation.

Evenings

The late shift is the busiest. Night duty starts at either 10pm or 11pm. A new shift comes on duty to deal with the turn out from the pubs. On busy nights officers from the earlier shift often stay on for a few hours to bolster the numbers. Prior to the legislation on 24 hour drinking most revellers were home and in bed by 2am. Now, with clubs obtaining extended drinking hours and the British culture of binge drinking, many of our young people are coming out of these clubs drunk, and often in no state to get home. Young men and women brawl in the street, often leading to criminal damage to property and in some circumstances serious injury.

Too much police time is spent dealing with this anti-social behaviour, leaving criminals free to travel through police districts unchallenged, as resources are directed to public order offences. There was a time when the police set up road checks to stop and search vehicles for stolen property, drugs and offensive weapons in the early hours of the morning. These road checks are now few and far between as front line officers are diverted to offences of anti social behaviour because of excessive drinking. Police forces need to be more proactive in detecting licensing offences. Clubs have gone unsupervised for too long, and have been flouting the licensing laws, by serving customers who are obviously drunk.

After the dust has settled and the streets are free from drunks, officers have an opportunity to patrol pro actively, looking for thieves and burglars. Working under the cover of darkness the criminal has considerable advantages, and police officers must know their ground well to detect their prey. Local intelligence will identify an area of persistent crime. Most criminals in cities work within a mile of their home address. Just like the fox, they will know their area intimately and move along back alleys, gardens and avenues looking for open windows, insecure doors, and valuable items left in cars. These can provide rich pickings for the night thief.

Chapter Ten
Recruitment, training and careers

The Selection Process

I N recent years careers in the police have become sought after. Difficulties in the general economy and the reduction in the size of the armed forces are contributing factors. The wide range of career paths available in the police broadens the appeal. There is the prospect of long term employment within the same organisation, reasonably good pay, a fairly early retirement age and attractive, state backed, pension benefits. All police forces in the UK have websites and there are adverts for all types of jobs available.

The police service can now afford to be selective. Many applicants have A-levels. Degrees are also common: 20% of the officers in the Metropolitan Police have them. There is now a preference for more mature recruits, who have seen a bit of life before joining the service. It can be an advantage to have been in the armed forces, to have worked as a PCSO or to have operated as a Special Constable.

Applicants attend a selection interview, take a written exam, undergo a medical and provide references to verify their good character.

Those accepted attend regional training centres (Hendon, in London) for about 20 weeks. This is reasonably demanding training, involving practical exercises and exams in criminal law and police procedure. Not everyone survives the process: the drop out rate is about 20%.

The next step for newly qualified constables (always in uniform at this early stage) is a probationary period working as a police officer, closely supervised by more experienced colleagues. Some of these will themselves be constables. Many officers spend long careers at this rank. Obviously they gain considerable experience (reflected in progressive pay increases) in the process.

Efforts are made to make the police broadly representative of the people they serve by recruiting from all ethnic and religious groups. The make up of the service has changed considerably as a result. However it remains the case that some communities are, for a variety of reasons, difficult recruiting grounds. Not all view the police favourably, or see a police career as a suitable one for young people.

In the last 20-30 years the proportion of female officers has greatly increased. They now comprise 20-25% of the force and undertake almost all types of police work. Some hold very senior positions.

Promotion

Promotion is not automatic at any stage in a police career. In common with most other walks of life it becomes more difficult higher up the structure – there are relatively few top jobs.

After about five years as a constable some are ready to seek to become Sergeants. This involves exams and evidence of suitable practical experience.

Promotion to Inspector can follow for those who have had at least three years experience as Sergeants – it is often considerably longer. This promotion is a significant transition and usually involves a move away from front line policing and towards a desk bound, management role. Inspectors are often in charge of four sergeants and 30-40 other officers.

For those who reach the rank of Chief Inspector, or higher, the transition from hands on police work to management functions is still more apparent. These senior office promotions are decided on assessment, and an individual's career path and achievements, including psychometric testing.

The system set up in the 1960's, whereby those who might be suitable for high rank were sent to Bramshill to attend the Special Course, survives in a modified form. People are selected at the rank of Sergeant and undertake a 12-month course, at the end of which they return to duty as Inspectors. Not all of them progress to glittering careers. Good quality mentoring by senior officers is required if relatively young Inspectors are to make a success of their command duties.

Ongoing career training

Chief Inspectors attend a residential course at the Bramshill Staff College, which covers much of the training offered to senior officers in England, Wales and Northern Ireland. This is the junior command course and lasts six weeks. Superintendants and above attend the senior officers command course. There is specialist training for still higher ranks, which covers such things as finance, the management of major incidents and the process of liaising with politicians who belong to Police Authorities.

Chapter Eleven
Major challenges

Theft of vehicles

THE organisation of major crime has moved away from armed robberies, which provided cash to invest in drugs, to the theft of high value cars. The main reason for the move to vehicle crime was the high penalties for armed robbery, and the low priority placed on the detection of motor vehicle crime by police forces.

Range Rovers, Porsches, Aston Martins, Ferraris, Bentleys and BMWs all fetch good money if exported overseas, with little risk to the organised criminal. All of the above cars can be altered and given new identities in foreign countries where the police do not have the technology to make the checks necessary to establish the true identity of a vehicle. A recent trip to South Africa revealed that UK criminals are exporting high value stolen cars to that country.

It must be said that the private sector has done a huge amount of work to provide additional security for vehicles to deter the criminal; however the criminal will always be one step ahead of the authorities as he counters the measures introduced by the manufacturers.

The security marking of property is an essential tool for deterring theft, both household property, plant machinery, and vehicles. Retainagroup is one leader in this market, with over 10 million vehicles marked. This type of vehicle marking allows the police to trace owners of the property and prosecute the thieves.

Drug related crime

The drugs trade is very lucrative. It is closely linked to the theft of cars, jewellery and other high value items. These can be exchanged for drugs in Europe and the Far East. The drugs are smuggled into the country and sold on, eventually making the criminal 40 times the value of the property stolen. Police forces have for the last 20 years focused on reducing the original thefts, rather than stopping the import of the drugs. There are victims of burglary, robbery, and car theft, but there is no direct victim when a drug supplier is arrested. (There are of course victims: all the users who become addicted and perpetuate the circle of crime). Clear ups for burglary, robbery, and car crime have been seen to be more important than the arrest and detection of drug suppliers.

This strategy has lead to an increase in gun crime in many major cities, as gangs tussle for territory to supply drugs. The problem of the supply of drugs is a continuing challenge for police forces. The rewards are such that as one dealer is taken out, another will readily fill their shoes. Every police area has a drug problem, whether it is cultivation in industrial units in small police areas such as Wiltshire, or the cutting and supply of drugs from inner city blocks of flats. Police officers have to be constantly alert for changing habits of local people and the furtive supply of drugs from street corners, pubs, and clubs.

Where drug supply is identified, police will collect intelligence, and in certain circumstances conduct surveillance on the suppliers. Evidence collected will include photographic and video evidence which, when presented at court, is often irrefutable. It is often expensive to obtain, with observations having to be conducted over many days. However when confronted with the evidence the offenders will often have to plead guilty, thus saving considerable sums of public money on legal aid and court time.

Sources of drugs

The Class B drug cannabis has a wide range of users, some of whom view it as a recreational drug, akin to alcohol. It is however illegal, partly because of significant concerns over its impact on health. Cannabis is often produced in the UK, where the plant can grow successfully. In more compact resin form it is often imported from the Caribbean by gangs.

Cocaine is produced in great quantities by powerful and ruthless gangs in South America. It can arrive in the UK via the Caribbean and other routes.

Heroin is grown, most notably, in Afghanistan, where many farmers are dependent on it for their livelihoods. Like Cocaine it is a Class A drug with strong addictive qualities.

The international drug trade, as a whole, is a multi-billion dollar industry with worldwide scope. Big sums of money, ingenuity, violence and corruption are used to produce and distribute drugs of all kinds.

The war on drugs is conducted in many ways and absorbs huge resources. Concerns about it are sometimes used as one of the arguments for military intervention in failed or problematic states, such as Afghanistan and certain parts of South and Central America. The Royal Navy regularly conducts anti drugs patrols in the Caribbean. Customs Officers (some of them armed) try to prevent drugs from entering the UK.

New types of drug

There is a strong market for things thought likely to deliver a kick or thrill, perhaps on a night out. Alcohol sales in certain venues can be surprisingly low, as pills of various kinds are consumed instead. Back street laboratories continually produce new ones. They may be very dangerous, but until they are identified and analysed they may be "off the radar", so far as the law is concerned and therefore, arguably, legal.

The impact of drugs

The drug trade, directly or indirectly, is undoubtedly a major driver of crime in many ways. At a high level it corrupts, up to and including politicians, top officials and in some cases entire governments. Hugely wealthy criminals involved in the trade are very hard to catch. Organised crime, spanning continents, derives much of its revenue from the drugs trade.

At street level there is an inexhaustible supply of people ready to undertake the risky task of supplying drug users. The turf wars between individuals or gangs that arise lead to many crimes of violence. They also contribute to a culture, even a way of life, where gang loyalty and an obsession with local "respect" displace interest in normal education or careers.

A drug habit can be expensive. Much theft and other crime is driven by people's need to fund it.

Legalise drugs?

The hugely expensive battle against the drug trade has undoubtedly achieved significant successes. Despite all the problems, arrests are made, sometimes of major figures. Impressive amounts of drugs are seized and destroyed every year. Nonetheless, this has been the pattern for many years and the trade goes on as vigorously as ever. Illicit drugs are now the third most valuable industry after food and oil: estimated at $450 billion a year, all in the control of criminals.

One idea occasionally talked about is to legalise the drug trade. If drugs were to be sold legally, perhaps by state run outlets, the revenues would not go to criminals and be available for governments instead, perhaps easing pressure on taxpayers. The most dangerous drugs could be sold in controlled conditions (e.g. clean needles could be supplied for injections) with health and other advice available to those who wanted it. Legalisation, it is sometimes said, would drain the lifeblood away from vast areas of criminal activity.

It is fifty years since the 1961 UN Single Convention of Narcotic Drugs was launched. There is a view that the global war on drugs has failed. Use of the major controlled drugs has risen, and supply is cheaper, purer, and more available than ever before. It is estimated that there are 250 million drug users.

The legalisation of drugs would take a huge burden of work from the police. It is estimated that 50% of all police work is related to drug related crime. There is pressure to consider legalisation. Even some senior police officers have argued for this.

Legalisation is unlikely. The weight of the law is firmly against harmful activities of a great many kinds, notably violence which injures people. Drug use hurts people, sometimes fatally.

Terrorism

There have been political movements which have come and gone over the years, where the police service has had to monitor and report to the government of the day. The Special Branch and the Anti Terrorist Branch in recent years have been proactive in protecting the public from Islamic fundamentalists, and before that the Provisional IRA. In addition to deterring and interrupting any terrorist intent, the police service is protecting the government of the day. Part of any terrorist strategy is to bring chaos to the streets of the capital and perhaps bring the government down. This threat, although real, has never got close to being successful.

Demonstrations and Riot control

There was a major re-think after the Brixton riots, in which unprotected officers confronted a mob throwing petrol bombs. The police now have dedicated teams to deal with such situations. London, as the capital city, is regularly chosen for demonstrations of various kinds. Approximately 3,000 take place there in a typical year.

Those organising demonstrations are required by law to inform the police. Specialist senior officers are trained to assess the associated risks and policing requirements. In almost all cases there is reasonable liaison with the organisers. The timing and route are agreed and arrangements made for communication with the organising stewards of the march.

Demonstrations

Demonstrations, particularly large ones, impose considerable burdens on the police and can cause disruption to others, as traffic flows and sometimes access to buildings are affected. They are of course part of our democratic way of life and nearly all of them proceed peacefully. Occasionally they get out of hand, exposing people to injury and buildings and other things to damage. This is criminal conduct to which the police need to respond.

There are now considerable specialist resources available, especially in London, to deal with rioting and major crowd control issues. The Metro-politan Police have about 800 "Level 1" officers with special training in this work. There is now a lot of protective clothing and other equipment that can be used: a far cry from the early 1980's. If necessary, support can be provided by other officers (at Levels 2 and 3) who have also received training in dealing with what can be highly charged and alarming situations.

These days every action is liable to be filmed, either by the formal media or on mobile phones. The resultant record can then be examined in detail and at leisure, in the days and weeks which follow. It will be carefully exam-ined by those anxious to criticise police actions. Sometimes the criticism is justified – police are human and can go too far, on the spur of the moment, in violent or threatening situations.

Some demonstrations are organised with the clear aim of causing trouble, damage and disruption. On other occasions an initially peaceful one is taken over by a violent minority. The police can try to anticipate this and plan accordingly. The tactics used (such as the so called "kettling" of groups, to prevent them from moving to other areas) can be criticised, or even reviewed by the courts. Criticism is easier to come by than realistic suggestions of alternative approaches. It is perhaps to the credit of the police that, at least in mainland UK, such things as tear gas, water cannon and rubber bullets have not been used, despite the fact that it has been necessary to deal with a number of major incidents in the heart of our capital city.

Riots

The riots in the summer of 2011 left many premises unprotected from groups of criminals intent on looting and committing arson. This brought home to the country just how thin the blue line of policing can be when the police service is put under pressure. Why was the police response so slow to tackle this violence, theft and criminal damage?

The thin blue line became very difficult to establish in the recent riots. A key factor was the multiple sites of disturbances. The use of social media networking sites to mobilise rioters in over a dozen locations meant that available resources became very stretched, as police boroughs responded by sending their officers to a location where there was trouble, only to find that they also came under attack.

Tactical requirements indicate that unless there is a threat to life, officers should act with restraint where they are clearly outnumbered. The arrest of rioters, many of whom are high on drink and drugs, puts the lives of police officers in danger. There are intelligence units on the ground filming the rioters, and there are many thousands of CCTV cameras filming the action.

The number of arrests eventually made (over 3,000 individuals) can be said to justify the approach used. However it is of grave concern that force mobilisation systems did not provide London with enough boots on the ground.

Major events

Events which attract large numbers of people, such as big football matches and royal weddings, involve considerations of crowd management and protection of a different kind.

There are long standing arrangements, based on hard experience, for the policing of football matches. Football hooliganism and straightforward overcrowding have led to big problems in the past. A whole series of measures, ranging from changing the timing of matches, the introduction of all seater stadiums and elaborate steps to identify key trouble makers have greatly improved matters in recent years. More families are now happy to attend big games.

Terrorism is a constant threat. For very big events, such as a royal wedding, much planning and other work goes on long in advance, to the extent of searching buildings, sealing manhole covers and assessing intelligence. Here the police work at high level with other agencies, including the armed forces.

The London Olympics of 2012 provided Britain the chance to welcome people from all over the world. Security considerations were to the fore and the measures taken included elaborate precautions as to the construction of the buildings.

Emergency planning

Every police force has a major incident room. This is not otherwise used and can become operational within an hour or so. It would then act as the base for dealing with the problem.

One of the duties of very senior, ACPO level, officers is to participate in the planning of the response to a wide variety of incidents and disasters. They may be natural calamities, accidents or the result of terrorism or even enemy activity. The planning process involves civil servants, the armed forces and other agencies (such as the other emergency services). Occasionally exercises are carried out to test the plans and the ability of the authorities to carry them out.

Anti-social behaviour

Academic studies and practical experience strongly suggest that environmental factors have a considerable impact on behaviour, including crime. Sheer common sense suggests that crime is less likely in pleasant conditions when people have enough money and plenty to do, compared to run down, deprived areas of high unemployment and limited facilities. It can be viewed as "the broken window syndrome". If there are broken windows in a street and they remain unrepaired, the chances of more windows getting broken greatly increase.

Some years ago The New York police, acting with other city authorities, adopted a "no tolerance" policy in respect of "minor crime", such as graffiti, litter and casual damage to property. Crime levels dropped significantly.

In the UK some very deprived areas seem stuck in a cycle of decline. Few people work and the environment is shabby. Few police forces have the resources to respond with an effective "no tolerance" policy. Efforts are made, via CPSO patrols, cooperation with social services departments and housing agencies and other initiatives.

Anti Social Behaviour Orders (ASBO's) can be imposed by Courts, without proof of a specific offence. They seek to prevent objectionable behaviour by imposing conditions on the recipient, breach of which is an offence. They are not a "magic bullet" so far as undesirable behaviour is concerned.

The police have to deal with society as it is. They cannot, themselves, solve all of its problems. Police action can result in offenders appearing in Court. Especially in the case of young offenders, this rarely removes them from the streets, where ASBO status can sometimes be a badge of honour!

Chapter Twelve

Prosecuting offenders

Offences

T HE police are responsible for investigating breaches of the criminal law. They are not alone in this. Various other authorities, including Customs, Local Authorities and the tax authorities regularly investigate and prosecute certain offences. It is also possible for private individuals to bring prosecutions, although this is rarely done.

A breach of the criminal law is an offence. The law only recognises an offence once there has been a conviction by a Court. Prior to that stage the accused person may be subject to some restrictions (such as bail conditions) or, in serious cases, kept in prison. He is nonetheless presumed to be innocent unless and until there is a conviction.

The law recognises that some offences (such as murder) are much more serious than others. Most cases are towards the lower end of the scale and are dealt with by Magistrates Courts. These often have lay people sitting as magistrates, instead of professional judges. More serious cases go to higher level Crown Courts. There are several levels of these. The most serious cases are dealt with by juries, whose task is to decide whether the prosecution case has been proved to the very high standard required in criminal cases. This requires them to be "sure" of the guilt of the accused.

The Crown Prosecution Service ('CPS')

Changes to the Criminal Justice system mean that the police no longer prosecute offenders. This responsibility has passed to the Crown Prosecution Service (the "CPS"). The Police and Criminal Evidence Act ("PACE") in 1984 brought this about, together with changes in the interviewing of prisoners, bail requirements, searching premises and stop and search. It was the biggest shake up of the criminal justice system since the formation of the police service.

The earlier system

Before these changes, the police dealt directly with a large number of the less serious cases. They decided whether or not to bring charges and what charges to bring. Police officers themselves often presented the prosecution case in the Magistrate's Court. There were some advantages to this system, which often resulted in cases being dealt with quickly. Now, minor cases, which would have been dealt with in a matter of weeks by the police, can take months to come to court. Often the punishment handed down comes so long after the commission of the offence that it loses its impact on the offender and, more importantly, the victim.

The changes introduced by PACE came about because of concerns that the police had too many roles to play, which occasionally led to abuse. They investigated offences, arrested suspects, questioned them, decided what charges to bring and then themselves prepared evidence for the Court and dealt with the prosecution on the day of the trial. It was common practice to seek to negotiate a guilty plea, which, if agreed to, saved considerable time and cost. All of this revolved around the local Magistrates Courts, sometimes (incorrectly) referred to as "Police Courts" – admittedly some of the older ones were close to the local police station.

The Crown Prosecution Service, which is staffed by specialist criminal lawyers employed as civil servants, receives reports and evidence from the police and decides whether or not to prosecute. There must be a good chance of securing a conviction. Many cases are clear cut. Some are much more evenly balanced. The involvement of the CPS staff means that some agency, other than the investigating police, takes an independent look at the case before deciding whether and how to proceed. Like all lawyers they can and should bring a degree of professional detachment to the task.

The decisions can be difficult. If the wrong charges are decided upon a case can get into difficulty and criminals escape the punishment they deserve, or get off too lightly because serious offences were not pursued.

One major problem with the CPS is that it struggles to cope with its caseload. The legal profession is a generally well paid one. Many good lawyers prefer the attractions of private practice to the Civil Service environment (and pay scales) of the CPS. It does not always attract the best legal brains. Like most organisations it would perform better if it was given more money and resources. As it is the relationship between the CPS and police can sometimes (but by no means always) be a strained one. Delays can be considerable, which means that a case can become stale, as the memories of witnesses, who may face vigorous questioning in court, start to fade. The CPS view of a case may differ from that of the investigating police officers. Cases which they have worked on for months may be dropped by the CPS, perhaps because of concerns about the prospects of success at trial.

Bringing criminal charges

If the CPS decides to charge someone, the charge or charges are set out carefully in writing and served on the defendant, who will, almost always, be advised by lawyers. Legal Aid (i.e. state funded payment of the legal fees) is often available to pay for this.

The task of the defence lawyers is to represent and advise the accused. Quite often the advice is that the prosecution case is so strong that a guilty plea makes sense. This is almost invariably rewarded by a reduced sentence. Sometimes a plea bargain can be negotiated with the CPS. In return for pleading guilty to a lesser offence the defendant is not prosecuted for more serious ones.

In cases which are defended, the CPS now organise the attendance of witnesses and presentation of evidence. The witnesses are often police officers. Most police give evidence many times in the course of their careers. It can be a daunting process: defence lawyers can be very robust in their questioning, up to and including suggestions that the police officer is lying, corrupt or incompetent. It can be important for the witness to stay calm and stick very carefully to the known facts. The English court procedure can be challenging but it has its good points. It normally produces the right result and is particularly good at avoiding wrongful convictions most of the time. The defendant gets the benefit of doubt.

Chapter Thirteen
The future

THE Police Service of England and Wales is under pressure to become more efficient. Because of general economic circumstances, money is short. Government has demanded greater efficiency. The challenge is to achieve a high quality service with a diminishing annual budget.

Reallocation of specialists

Over the past twenty years, many specialist departments have been set up to detect a variety of offences, including the cultivation and supply of drugs, domestic violence, robbery, paedophile offences and many others. These departments have removed experienced front line officers and supervisors to these specialist duties. Police forces under budget pressures will have to decide whether to continue with so many specialist teams or return many officers to core policing. Any reduction in the numbers of police officers may see police forces sharing specialist departments in order to put more boots on the streets to prevent and detect crime.

One problem with too much specialisation is that crime does not always fit tidily into neat little specialised areas. It is sometimes necessary to step back and have a general overview of what is going on. Serious criminals may be up to several different things at once.

Too much specialisation can also prevent the development of versatile, rounded officers with the broad experience needed to make them suitable for command positions. An overly specialist officer may find himself stuck at a relatively low rank.

Reorganisation

The structure of the police service needs to be considered. Does England

and Wales need 43 police forces, with all the hierarchy, and costs involved? Is it time to amalgamate many of the smaller forces, some of which have only a thousand police officers?

The argument for the present system is local accountability. However can the country ignore the pressures of diminishing budgets? Police forces are already adjusting the response times to emergency calls upwards from 12 minutes to 15 minutes in the light of a reduction in police officer numbers. The proposal made in 1964 to form ten regions should be considered again. Larger police forces would allow for greater flexibility in the deployment of resources and reduce duplication. The number of control rooms managing 999 calls could be reduced to a few Regional Control Centres. The Metropolitan Police, with 32,000 police officers, has moved away from 64 divisional controls to three control rooms, and the service to the public has been maintained.

Streamlined procedures

The Government's aim to reduce the time that officers spend at their desks is welcomed by police forces. Too much emphasis has been put on meeting targets, and completing paperwork. There are still too many tasks being done in the old, labour intensive, ways. Giving notice of prosecution to offenders by registered mail, rather than via a police officer, is an example of one sensible way of saving police time. After all, members of the public have received posted notices of intended prosecution for speeding for years.

There is likely to be even more effort to ensure that any tasks that can be performed by civilian members of staff are dealt with by them. They are usually cheaper to employ than police officers.

Modern communications and technology, in the form of hand held devices and those mounted in vehicles, reduce the need to visit police stations in the course of a shift. Their capabilities will no doubt continue to improve. Further integration of different systems should reduce the need to input information more than once.

There is already an enormous amount of information available to the police, spread across a great many different databases and other sources. Integration of systems with a common data format will increase inter operability between police forces, and eventually lead to regionalization.

The Police that we deserve

Although viewed by some as a very visible arm of the state, responsible for the enforcement of its laws, police officers are drawn from society and are themselves part of it. They are not a separate caste, or military style force.

Maintaining quality in a time of rapid change and shortage of money will be very challenging. In many ways the calibre and standing of police officers has improved over the years, at least if this is judged by their educational attainment and the pay and conditions that they enjoy. There is less temptation to succumb to the odd "backhander", as in the old days of low pay and very long hours.

Consider the alternatives to the British system. One only has to travel to parts of Europe to see the military style of policing, or to Russia, where there is still an element of State Policing. Corruption is rife in many poorer countries, where police officers have to supplement their meagre income with on the spot "fines", usually taken in American dollars.

Society gets the police force that it deserves. The British police are not perfect. However the country can feel proud of them. It is hard to identify anywhere else with a better police service.

Where to find out more

www.homeoffice.gov.uk/police A great deal of information can be accessed from this, the Home Office website

Each police force has its own website. Examples are: The Metropolitan Police Service: www.contact.met.police.uk/home

www.gmp.police.uk The Greater Manchester Police

www.wiltshire.police.uk Wiltshire Police

www.npia.police.uk/en/8934.htm Link to the DNA database

www.polfed.org The Police Federation represents most officers

www.acpo.police.uk Information about very senior officers

There are numerous organisations which campaign in the general field of the protection of human rights and the operation of the legal system. One of the best known is Liberty: www.liberty-human-rights.org.uk

About the author

I AN JAMES served with the Metropolitan Police for 30 years. He worked in several specialist departments during his career, serving with the Traffic Division, the Special Patrol Group and the Territorial Support Group in South London. Other postings included Hornsey, Streatham and Epsom police divisions.

Later he was a senior manager at the Central Command Complex, managing the 999 call handling department at New Scotland Yard. At the end of his career he was part of a police team that designed and developed a national 999 call handling computer application for the UK Police Service.

During his service he attended Exeter University and obtained a Masters Degree in Police Studies.

On retirement Ian started a consultancy company. He works closely with the Emergency Services and the Ministry of Defence, designing control rooms. He writes business cases for leading security companies in the UK, and works with suppliers in the emergency control room market.

Ian has represented the Metropolitan Police Motor Club Internationally, rallying a BMW 2002 and a BMW M3. He finished both the London to Mexico Rally and the London to Sydney Rally.

More titles in the Quicklook series

You can find out more about our wide range of titles at **quicklookbooks.com**

Quicklook at Police

The British police have pioneered many aspects of policing. We explore how and why and how the service is shaping up to the 21st century. We find out about the many different skills and departments and how they fit together.

Quicklook at Pensions

This clear, layman friendly, book is a must read for anyone looking for a "spin free" guide to pensions.

Quicklook at Management

Every organisation needs to be managed. Part art, part science, part seat of the pants, there are many approaches. This up to date book covers the main ideas.

Quicklook at Education

This guide to the vital subject of education covers the system from pre-school to post graduate, exams and qualifications, the teaching professions and theories of learning.

Quicklook at Movies

This brings the world of film to life as we explore the characters that shaped and starred in it, the technology which developed it, the many different types of film and the booms and busts of an industry sometimes as dramatic as anything on screen.

Quicklook at Business

This is the most comprehensive short guide to the business world that you are likely to find.

Quicklook at Marketing

Marketing affects us all. It is crucial to business success. What is it and how does it work? Experienced marketing expert Patrick Forsyth unwraps its mysteries. You launch a new product.

Quicklook at Defence

Defence is vital and often in the news. How does it operate in a time of new challenges and tight budgets? Command a crisis operation.

Quicklook at Human Resources

This is a must for anyone interested in a job or the world of work.

Quicklook at Accountancy

All of the basics are covered, from the key elements of accounts and the ways in which they are used. Accountancy is the backbone of most organisations. It is itself a huge industry. We look at the main players, how it works and the many career options.

Quicklook at India

An emerging superpower, India embraces many different peoples, languages and religions. Nowhere has older or deeper cultures, or so much diversity.

Quicklook at Dogs

There are over seven million dog owners in the UK. Find out why we share such a strong bond with our canine companions.

Quicklook at Wine

Wine is a luxury enjoyed by many, but understood by few. This book gets you to grips with the subject, from grapes to glass.

Quicklook at Vets

Millions of us care for animals and vets are familiar and reassuring figures. Find out about the tremendous scope of their work.

Quicklook at Flying

How has flying developed? How does a plane work? What is happening in aviation now? What will happen in the future? What does it take to be a pilot?

Quicklook at Property

Property (real estate) is the ultimate base for wealth and the economy. It comes in many forms. Many jobs depend on it. Learn how the world of property operates.

Quicklook at Medicine

Medicine provides more and more remedies, often vital to life. What is becoming possible? How is it done? How does the body work? Find out about the medical professions. Be a GP for a day.

Quicklook at Law

English Law has spread its influence to many countries. Why? How does it work? How is it changing? How does the legal profession operate? Get inside a Court case.